THEY SAW THE LORD

THEY SAW THE LORD

by

BONNELL SPENCER, O.H.C.

*Then were the disciples glad, when
they saw the Lord.*

ST. JOHN 20:20

Morehouse-Barlow Co., Inc.
Wilton, Connecticut

Morehouse-Barlow Co., Inc.
78 Danbury Road
Wilton, Connecticut 06897

ISBN 0-8192-1332-2

Library of Congress Catalog Card Number 83-61765

Printed in the United States of America

To my
FATHER and MOTHER
who, by word and example,
were to me
the first witnesses
of the
Risen Christ.

Preface

This book originated in the recataloging of a library. When we arranged the devotional books by subject-matter, we discovered that, whereas there were several shelves of books on our Lord's Passion and Death, there was but a handful of volumes on His Resurrection. This raised in my mind the question whether or not some of the weakness of modern Christianity might be due to that disproportion of emphasis.

Concluding that the neglect of the Resurrection is a source of spiritual loss, I resolved to do what little I could to remedy the situation. The result is this attempt to consider thoughtfully and prayerfully the Bible accounts of the Resurrection Appearances and to draw from them a deeper faith in the Risen Christ and a clearer realization of our potential relationship with Him here and now.

Naturally, there is much in the content of this book which is not original. But since its ideas and insights have been picked up over the years from many books, sermons, lectures, and conversations, I am no longer able, for the most part, to identify their sources. The few instances where it is possible for me to give credit have been noted in the text. To the others I can give only this general expression of my indebtedness and gratitude.

I must, however, make special mention of the encouragement I have received from the Rev. Alan Whittemore,

Superior of the Order of the Holy Cross, and of the valuable suggestions that he and the Rev. John Baldwin, O.H.C., have given.

The second chapter appeared in *The Holy Cross Magazine*, April, 1946, under the title, "The Empty Tomb."

Bonnell Spencer, O.H.C.

Preface to New Edition

It is a joy and privilege to have one's first book reprinted. But it also has its embarrassments. If one has been truly alive for the past thirty-five years, one's outlook has changed. So has the world and the Church. Details that seemed important in 1947 now appear quaint and irrelevant. I said to a friend, when the reprint was being considered, "I could not have written it today." His reply was apt, "You don't have to; you already have." And we agreed that it presents material which is still meaningful in a readable form.

Among the aspects which I feel are outdated is the attempt to consider the details of the resurrection accounts to be historical, as we use that adjective today. I now see such an approach is unfair to the evangelists. They were not newspaper reporters accurately recording the trivia of ephemeral events. They were trying to present, as vividly as possible, the eternal significance of Jesus' life, death, and resurrection. To that end, in terms of the criteria of their day, they were allowed what we should consider great license in handling, embroidering, and perhaps even inventing, the stories they used to communicate that truth.

But when those narratives are taken as the basis for expounding the principal elements of the spiritual life, the fit still seems to me remarkable. The primary purpose of the book, which originated in a series of retreat addresses given to a Community of Sisters, was to review the spiritual journey. The ease with which the resurrection accounts could be used for that purpose goes to show that, for history and for us, the spiritual significance of Jesus the Christ "is the same yesterday, today, and forever."

— Bonnell Spencer, O.H.C.
Pentecost 1983

Contents

Chapter		Page
	Preface	vii
	Preface to New Edition	ix
I.	The Keynote of the Gospel	1
II.	What the World Saw	14
III.	The Disciple Whom Jesus Loved	28
IV.	The Faithful Follower	42
V.	The Penitent	56
VI.	The Way of Prayer	69
VII.	The Church at Worship	83
VIII.	Spiritual Combat	97
IX.	God's Little Ones	111
X.	The Way of the Cross	123
XI.	The Virgin Mother	136
XII.	Rule and Governance	148
XIII.	Apostolate	161
XIV.	He Was Taken Up	176
XV.	The Heavens Opened	189
XVI.	Born Out of Due Time	201
XVII.	The Judgment	215

I

The Keynote of the Gospel

Ye men of Israel, hear these words; Jesus of Nazareth, a man approved of God among you by miracles and wonders and signs, which God did by him in the midst of you, as ye yourselves also know: Him, being delivered by the determinate counsel and foreknowledge of God, ye have taken, and by wicked hands have crucified and slain: Whom God hath raised up, having loosed the pains of death: because it was not possible that he be holden of it. . . . This Jesus hath God raised up, whereof we all are witnesses.

ACTS 2:22-24, 32.

"This Jesus hath God raised up, whereof we all are witnesses." These words are the climax and theme of the first Christian sermon, which Peter addressed to the crowd on Whitsunday morning. He repeated them almost verbatim in his subsequent sermons and in his testimony before the Jewish authorities. Clearly, he believed the Resurrection of Christ to be the keynote of the Gospel. He singled it out for primary emphasis and counted on it to convince others, as it had already convinced him, that Jesus was "both Lord and Christ." Nor was he disappointed. Many in the crowd responded to his sermon by asking the Apostles, "Men and brethren, what shall we do?" and about three thousand received Baptism on that same day.

1

The Apostles considered that the characteristic function of their office was to give eye-witness testimony to the Resurrection of Christ. When, ten days earlier, Peter had asked the others to choose a man to "take part of this ministry and apostleship, from which Judas by transgression fell," they selected Joseph and Matthias, who had been with Jesus "unto that same day that he was taken up," that is, until the Ascension. They were eligible because they had seen the Risen Christ. Matthias was chosen by lot and "ordained to be a witness . . . of [Christ's] Resurrection."

We can easily understand why that event loomed so large in the Apostles' thought. It had transformed their lives and made the preaching of the Gospel possible. On Holy Saturday, they had been the victims of grief-stricken fear. On Easter, all was changed. St. John tells us, with masterful understatement, "Then were the disciples glad, when they saw the Lord." Death had not ended their association with Him. It had raised it to a higher, more glorious, more intimate plane. Wonderful as His friendship in Galilee had been, it took on a new significance now that He had risen from the grave. Forty days of intermittent Resurrection Appearances convinced them that Christ's work on earth, far from being finished, was just beginning. The termination of the Appearances with the Ascension did not plunge them into grief. They understood enough by then to realize that, although they would see His face on earth no more, He was not leaving them. He would be with them always, even unto the end of the world. He would give them the power and guidance they needed to carry out the work He had for them to do. On Whitsunday, they received the Holy Spirit and began forthwith to proclaim the Good News that God had raised Jesus from the dead.

The Resurrection also gave them a Gospel to preach. Without that experience, they would have been able to tell men only of the tragedy which had occurred on Calvary. A Prophet mighty in deed and word had lived on earth. He had told men of the beauty of God's love and held out to them the hope of salvation. A few had heeded Him, but the leaders of God's Chosen People had surrendered Him to the Romans to mock, to scourge, and to crucify. Had this been the end of the story, it would have indicated that God's final effort to save man had failed. God Himself could not overcome such impenitence and hardness of heart. Man had had and had lost his last chance. The Christian message would have been one of despair.

The Resurrection was Christ's vindication. It revealed His triumph over sin and death. He had not been defeated and killed. He had laid down His life for the world. Now He had taken it up again that He might reap the harvest His sacrifice had won. At last, the disciples were able to understand His purpose. They recognized who He was. He was not only the Messiah. He was the Lamb of God that taketh away the sins of the world. He was the Lord of life and of death. Hardly daring to believe, they fell on their knees and worshiped Him as God.

Only the Resurrection could have opened their eyes to His divinity. They were Jews, trained in a monotheism which, in its exaltation of the One God, had increasingly thought of Him as remote. For them to realize that God Himself had come among them as a Man required a tremendous revolution in their whole pattern of thought. As

it was, though they recognized Him and treated Him as
God, praying to Him and worshiping Him, there are sur-
prisingly few direct references to His divinity in the New
Testament. This would seem to indicate that the early
Christians hesitated to express themselves dogmatically on
the subject. They found it hard to put into words the rec-
onciliation of His divine nature with the Unity of God. It
took the Church three centuries, under the guidance of the
Holy Spirit, to work out a satisfactory formula, the doctrine of the Trinity with its differentiation of the Three
Persons in the One God. Yet this formula, when found, expressed no more than the truth revealed to the Apostles
when they saw the Risen Lord. He was "declared to be the
Son of God with power . . . by the Resurrection from the
dead."

The Resurrection transformed the disciples into the
Church, the Body of Christ. He reunited them to Himself
and sent them forth to be His agents in the world. Because
they were in vital contact with Him they could preach in
His name. He is the Mind of the Church, speaking through
the Apostles and their successors in every generation, proclaiming the Good News of man's redemption. The Risen
Christ acts through His Body the Church to incorporate
souls into it by the water of Baptism. Through the Church,
He continues His ministry, forgiving sin, healing the sick,
comforting the afflicted, feeding men with His Body and
Blood. Because the Apostles had witnessed the Resurrection, they knew that they had more to give men than the
teachings of a dead Master. They could introduce men to
Christ Himself, living, ascended, and acting through them
to draw the world to His heart.

Fellowship with the Risen Christ was for them and is for us the source of power for the Christian life. We live "in Christ." "Know ye not," asks St. Paul, "that so many of us as were baptized into Jesus Christ were baptized into his death? Therefore we are buried with him by Baptism into death: that like as Christ was raised up from the dead by the glory of the Father, even so we also should walk in newness of life. For if we have been planted together in the likeness of his death, we shall be also in the likeness of his Resurrection." We are able to "put on the Lord Jesus Christ, and make not provision for the flesh, to fulfil the lusts thereof." Since we are risen with Christ we can "seek those things which are above, where Christ sitteth on the right hand of God." Our "life is hid with Christ in God."

Not only does the Risen Christ give us the power we need for this life. He assures us of our participation in the life to come. He is the Firstfruits of the Resurrection from the dead. Because He is risen, those who die united to Him will rise also. "Everyone which seeth the Son, and believeth on him, may have everlasting life:" our Lord promised, "and I will raise him up again at the last day. . . . I am the Resurrection, and the Life: he that believeth in me, though he were dead, yet shall he live." As St. Peter tells us, God "hath begotten us again unto a lively hope by the Resurrection of Jesus Christ from the dead."

The Resurrection is the keynote of the Christian message. Without it, there would have been no Christian Gospel, no Christian Faith, no Christian Church, no Christian life, no Christian hope. It revealed to the Apostles, and through them to us, the glorious truth of our redemption. It is the proof of God's victory over sin and death. It is the source of our power to know and follow Christ. Were doubt as to the Resurrection possible, the whole Christian position would be undermined. "If Christ be not risen," wrote St. Paul, "then is our preaching vain, and your faith is also vain. . . . Ye are yet in your sins. . . . If in this life only we have hope in Christ, we are of all men the most miserable."

The Church intends that the fact of Christ's Resurrection shall be held constantly before our eyes. All four Gospels culminate in that event. Three of them devote at least a chapter to exact accounts of the Appearances of the Risen Lord, relating them with a wealth of realistic detail. Even the slight inconsistencies in the narratives, such as we should expect to find in the testimony of eye-witnesses, serve only to validate their accuracy. St. Mark's Gospel, since its original ending is presumably lost, indicates but does not describe the Resurrection. So strongly did the early Church feel that this left the Gospel intolerably incomplete that a summary of the Appearances was compiled and added to it to take the place of the lost ending.

The Epistles refer to the Resurrection again and again, treating it, as we have seen, as the basis of our hope and the source of our power. The Book of Revelation shows us the Risen Christ in glory. The Creeds feature the Resurrection as the climax of the work of God the Son. "The third day he rose again from the dead: He ascended into heaven, And sitteth on the right hand of God the Father Almighty: from thence he shall come to judge the quick and the dead." Not content with all this, the Church has constructed her liturgical year with the Resurrection as its center. Advent, Christmas, Epiphany, Lent, Passiontide all lead up to the great Forty Days of Eastertide, the queen of seasons, followed by the continuation of the note of triumphant joy in Ascensiontide and Pentecost. Lest even this be not enough, Sunday has been instituted as a weekly commemoration of Easter and is kept as a feast even during the penitential seasons of Advent and Lent. Whatever else in the Gospel we may forget or neglect, the Church is determined that it shall not be the fundamental truth that "this Jesus hath God raised up."

Nevertheless, in spite of these precautions, there has been in western Christianity over the centuries a gradual shift of emphasis away from the Resurrection. The great masters of the spiritual life in every generation have protested against this tendency and have urged generous souls to pass beyond the initial stages of penitence and routine prayer to the heroic virtues attainable by the power of the Risen Lord. Saints have blazed the trail in seeking those things which are above. Still it is true that the main concern of the Church has been to induce the average Christian to perform those minimum duties whereby he may be saved.

In theology, the Atonement, the work done by Christ on the Cross, and the way in which we benefit by it, has provided the subject most stimulating to speculation and controversy. In practical matters, the determination of what is the least a Christian is required to do in terms of his obligation to God, the definition of what constitutes sin, the effort to produce penitence and conversion have absorbed the attention and energy of the Church. In popular devotion, the Passion has superseded the Resurrection as the center of interest. Meditation on the sufferings of Christ rather than on the glories of His Risen Life has been the chief stimulus to piety. The crucifix and "the old rugged cross" are the commonest Christian symbols. Lent has replaced Eastertide as the major season of devotion. In short, salvation from sin instead of life in union with the Risen Christ is the goal toward which the average earnest Christian is striving.

The results of this shift of emphasis have been disastrous. Christianity has been presented mainly as a negative process, an escape from sin. In view of this, outsiders can hardly be blamed when they accuse Christians of being escapists. Far too often we have fluctuated between overconcern with our poor sick souls and pharisaic complacency over our moral rectitude and conventional piety. Consequently, the world looks upon our religion as a quest for dull respectability and is not impressed by it. Lacking the triumphant power which can be obtained only by a constant and intimate fellowship with the living Christ, we are so ineffectual that the world can afford to disregard us. Except when society sinks to the final stages of degradation, as it did recently in Germany and Japan, there is no attempt at persecution. Most of the time, the world either ignores Christianity with contemptuous scorn or insults it with indifferent lip-service. Much as men and women crave salvation today, most of them are not inclined to accept the brand offered by the Church, for it seems too humdrum and anemic. They do not see in us any of the heroic joy and invincible strength which would be ours if we had put on the Lord Jesus. We do not reveal to men the Risen Christ. Instead, we hide Him from their eyes. We appear at best to be trying unsuccessfully to follow the teachings of a long-dead Master, a good Man, no doubt, but a weak and pathetic Victim of a miscarriage of justice.

Recently, a woman who is a faithful Church member took a problem to her rector. She had told her six-year-old son how Jesus had died on the cross. He remarked, "If Jesus is God's Son, why did God let that happen to him?"

"I did not know what to answer," admitted the woman.

"Did you tell him what happened on Easter?" asked the rector.

"I never thought of that."

There is the tragedy of modern Christianity. We think too seldom of the Resurrection. We have almost forgotten the Risen Christ. So little contact do we have with Him that we half believe we can dispense with Him altogether. When people calling themselves Christians doubt or deny that Jesus rose from the dead, as many do today, we are neither shocked nor surprised. If they can put forward a convincing case, we are tempted to admit that they may be right. We seem blissfully unaware that the Resurrection is the corner-stone of the Gospel and that, if it is pried loose, the whole of Christianity falls in ruins to the ground.

We are in mortal danger of succumbing to the modern attack on the basis of our faith and hope because we are too apathetic to defend ourselves against it. Just how valid are the current arguments which claim to prove that the Resurrection did not take place? Superficially, they seem impressive. Their exponents are men of learning who hold prominent and respected positions in various Christian bodies. Their case is supposed to rest on the impartial conclusions of painstaking scholarship. Is it possible that they are right and that the Church for nineteen centuries has been wrong in asserting that Jesus rose from the dead?

A closer examination of their arguments, however, reveals some major weaknesses. To begin with, whereas they all agree in denying the historicity of the Resurrection, the methods by which they handle the biblical evidence are amazingly varied and contradictory. Each scholar has his own theory, and when placed side by side, these theories cancel each other out. One, for instance, essays to prove that our Lord's body remained in the tomb, and hence, the Resurrection did not occur. Another, with equal confidence, claims to demonstrate that the body was surreptitiously removed, and then proceeds to the same conclusion. We begin to smell a rat. Is it not strange that mutually contradictory ways of interpreting the same evidence have led all these learned gentlemen to the same conclusion? Should not the grounds for a common conclusion be the same in every case? Is it not more likely, therefore, that their denial of the Resurrection rests on some line of thought which has nothing to do with the New Testament evidence, and that, having arrived at that conclusion, each of them is trying to dispose of the evidence against it as best he can?

This is precisely what has happened. Long before they open their Bibles, these scholars have decided that Jesus did not rise from the grave. The grounds for this conclusion are to be found in the prevailing atmosphere of modern thought, which is a pseudo-scientific materialism with its corollary that miracles do not happen. Consequently, a miracle like that of the Resurrection could not have taken place, no matter how strong the evidence for it may be. With this conviction firmly planted in their minds, they make their "impartial" examination of the New Testament accounts. In technical language, which is as impressive as it is incomprehensible to the layman, they prove to their own satisfaction that the Bible means the exact opposite of what it says. Unfortunately for their position, none of their explanations ever satisfies anyone except its author.

The irony of it is that, in their frantic efforts to avoid the miracle of the Resurrection, they have taken refuge in a far greater miracle. They ask us to believe that the Church, which has survived and prospered for two thousand years, originated in a colossal mistake. In asserting that God raised up Jesus, the Apostles were either fabricating a deliberate lie or suffering from a hysterical delusion. Is it not an amazing miracle that an institution conceived in falsehood should have had a vitality which has enabled it to outlast the fall of empires, to survive its own periods of weakness and corruption, and to be today the strongest force in the modern world? The millions of men and women who have believed that they heard the Risen Christ speak through the Church and found Him in sacraments and prayer have been deceived. There is no Risen Christ for them to know. Yet, in the strength of that delusion, they have left home and country to follow Christ, have given up comforts and possessions to serve Him, have endured torture and death rather than deny Him. These are extraordinary, not to say immoral, miracles compared with which the Resurrection of Christ is far simpler and more credible.

It is not the purpose of this book to refute in detail those who deny the Resurrection. We leave that to Christian

scholars, of whom there are many, who are competent to
answer them on their own grounds with their own weapons.
Our purpose is to counteract their influence by reminding
ourselves of what the Church tells us about the Resurrection of Christ. Accordingly, we shall let the Bible accounts
speak for themselves. We shall assume that they are accurate and try to see what they say happened. We shall not
hesitate to call on tradition and our own imagination to
sketch in the details and draw out their significance. This
may help to make the story more vivid. Yet we shall differ-
entiate between the first-hand accounts and our own
guesses, so that those who do not find the latter helpful
may disregard them. If by retelling the story we succeed in
showing that the New Testament narratives, considered
individually and in relation to each other, give us a consistent and plausible picture of a historical event, our first
purpose will have been achieved.

Our second purpose grows naturally out of the first.
Since as Christians we are called not only to believe that
Christ rose, but also to know Him, we shall endeavor to
find illustrated in the Appearances of the Risen Christ the
basic pattern of the spiritual life by which He comes to us.
We shall never forget that the Resurrection Appearances
were unique. In them, our Lord's Risen Body was seen and
handled by the disciples. Their purpose was to establish
the fact that He truly had risen from the tomb. Once this
purpose was fulfilled, the Appearances ceased. Even the
original disciples had to carry on for the rest of their lives
without a recurrence of them. On the basis of a faith born
of that experience and nourished by the ordinary channels
of grace, they had to serve and preach Christ. All other

Christians are called to know Him on the basis of the Apostles' testimony and to receive the blessing reserved for those who "have not seen, and yet have believed."

Still, the disciples were men and women like us. Our Lord had to approach them in terms of that human nature which we have in common with them. Therefore we should expect to find in the Resurrection Appearances the basic principles of the spiritual life, writ large and on a higher plane, that apply to our relationship with Christ. We shall do well to detect these principles. In the light of them, we shall be able the more readily to lay hold by faith on the all-important truth that "this Jesus hath God raised up," and thereby be equipped to fulfil our Christian vocation which is, by word and example, to be witnesses to the Risen Lord.

II

What the World Saw

Now the next day, that followed the day of the preparation, the chief priests and Pharisees came together unto Pilate, saying, Sir, we remember that that deceiver said, while he was yet alive, After three days I will rise again. Command therefore that the sepulchre be made sure until the third day, lest his disciples come by night, and steal him away, and say unto the people, He is risen from the dead: so the last error shall be worse than the first. Pilate said unto them, Ye have a watch: go your way, make it as sure as ye can. So they went, and made the sepulchre sure, sealing the stone, and setting a watch.

ST. MATTHEW 27:62-66.

And, behold, there was a great earthquake: for the angel of the Lord descended from heaven, and came and rolled back the stone from the door, and sat upon it. His countenance was like lightning, and his raiment white as snow: And for fear of him the keepers did shake, and became as dead men. . . . Some of the watch came into the city, and shewed unto the chief priests all the things that were done. And when they were assembled with the elders, and had taken counsel, they gave large money unto the soldiers, saying, Say ye, His disciples came by night, and stole him away while we slept. And if this come to the governor's ears, we will persuade him, and secure you. So they took the money, and did as they were taught: and this saying is commonly reported among the Jews until this day.

ST. MATTHEW 28:2-4, 11-15.

The conspiracy had succeeded magnificently. Powerful groups had felt their position threatened. Ordinarily these groups were at swords' points with each other. But although they had been moved by quite different motives and had proceeded along independent lines, their plots had dovetailed perfectly. The threat had been removed, and in such a way as to leave nothing to be desired by any of the groups concerned. Seldom have human schemes been crowned with such complete success.

The Pharisees had saved religion. They were the spiritual leaders of Israel. That Galilean Rabbi, who had taught so beautifully and so boldly, was recognized at once as a very dangerous Man. He did not respect their authority. He brushed aside some of their cherished traditions by which they had hedged the Law. He had even called them hypocrites. There was no good arguing with Him. He was too clever. They were no match for Him. When they set traps for Him, He had an uncanny knack of springing the traps on their own fingers.

The common people immensely enjoyed His discomfiture of the Pharisees. Crowds were following Him around the countryside, marveling at His miracles, hanging on His words. Something had to be done quickly. All the world had gone after Him. Soon the Pharisees would be laughed out of their position of authority and respect. Already, people snickered when the Pharisees took the chief seats in the synagog. The Law of Moses was at stake. Was not this the Law of the Most High God?

This false teacher must be eliminated. Yet death was not enough. If He died a hero, He might be considered a martyr. He must be discredited at the same time. Well, He had been. He had been condemned as a blasphemer and had suffered the curse of the Law, "Cursed is everyone that hangeth on a tree."

The Sadducees had saved the nation. They were the party of the High Priest. They had sold out to the Roman Empire. In exchange, they were recognized as Israel's native rulers and were allowed to operate the lucrative temple trade. The Galilean had attacked their vested interests. He had driven out their licensed merchants and money-changers. He had talked vaguely about destroying the Temple. Worst of all, He had made a triumphal entry into the city and allowed the people to hail Him as the Messiah. At any moment, the crowd might rise in revolt and crown Him king. Then Rome would clamp down. The last vestiges of independence would be swept away.

The Sadducees decided that it was expedient "that one man should die for the people, and that the whole nation perish not." The people must be saved from a foolhardy revolt and the inevitable reprisals. The Temple, the glory of Israel, must be defended. "They took counsel together for to put Him to death." How perfectly they had succeeded! There was even a delightful irony in the manner of His death. He who had called them robbers was Himself crucified between two thieves.

Pilate had saved the peace, the great *Pax Romana* which was the corner-stone of Roman policy. Rome was willing to grant considerable local autonomy as long as the peace was kept. What she would not tolerate was revolt. The local governor's chief responsibility was to forestall one. Pilate had come from Caesarea to Jerusalem at the always dangerous time of the Passover to see that no riots took place.

That year, it looked for a while as if a riot were inevitable. The party that gathered about the Galilean was potentially dangerous. As far as Pilate could see, the dispute centered largely around the Jews' religious customs. These in themselves did not interest him. But there must be no fighting over them among the Jews, and the rumors that the new Leader had kingly aspirations were ominous.

Pilate was pleased at the commendable quietness with which the arrest was effected. To be sure, he would have preferred not to have been called in on the case at all. He saw at once that the Prisoner was innocent, and hesitated to condemn Him. Yet even his effort to shift the responsibility to another's shoulders, though it failed of its first purpose, had borne good fruit. Herod was so flattered by having the Prisoner sent to him that he and Pilate were reconciled over a long-standing quarrel.

In the end, Pilate saw that the only way to save the peace was to condemn the Galilean. He did, and washed his hands of the whole affair. It had been a peaceful Passover after all. Caesar would be well pleased. Perhaps a promotion would be forthcoming.

Everybody was satisfied. Jesus was dead and buried. His followers were scattered; His cause discredited. The threat to the vested interests was removed. They were free once more to go their own way unmolested.

They were taking no chances, however. A great stone had been rolled against the door of the sepulchre. The next day, with Pilate's permission, seals were affixed. A watch was set. Nothing was overlooked. There would be no untoward occurrences, no embarrassing aftermath. Jesus was going to remain safely buried and forgotten.

And all the while, God "was in the world . . . and the world knew him not. He came unto his own, and his own received him not." They had not meant to reject God, of course. They knew not what they did. Their conscious and admitted motives were the highest. They were defending God's Law, God's Chosen People, God's Temple, yes, God's peace. Yet, in the process they crucified God.

This startling paradox is not difficult to resolve. They had identified God's interests with their own. Having started by asserting, "God's enemies are my enemies," they had imperceptibly drifted into the attitude, "My enemies are God's enemies." The process is very simple and has been repeated in every age. Pride infects a man's desire to serve God. It bids him think he can do something for God, depending on his own strength and devices. Gradually the interest shifts from God's will to the plans for serving Him. Before long the man is jockeying for position and authority that he may the more effectively carry out his schemes. Pride takes over more and more territory, until at last the original desire to serve God has become but the cloak to cover a selfish lust for power. Thus man usurps the place of God and in the name of religion or of the good life serves and exalts himself.

This is what had happened in Palestine. The Pharisees' zeal for the Law had concentrated more and more on the man-made hedges designed to protect it. The erection and cultivation of these hedges was the exclusive prerogative of the scribes and Pharisees. This was the basis of their authority and position. When our Lord attacked these man-made obstructions to the fulfilment of the Law, the Pharisees felt themselves attacked and turned on Him.

The Sadducees' zeal for the nation and the Temple was similarly contaminated by their desire for power and wealth. The *Pax Romana* had long since degenerated from a sincere effort to establish peace and trade throughout the world to a despotic and luxurious tyranny. Thus man organized the world to suit his selfish desires. Though it was done in the name of God, there was no room left for God in it. When He came He was a disturbing element which had to be eliminated.

But God did not remain eliminated. At the very moment when man felt most secure in his arrogant success, God reasserted Himself. Suddenly, in the darkness before the dawn, there was a mighty earthquake. The stone was rolled away from the door of the sepulchre. The soldiers, terrified, beheld—not the Risen Christ as is often portrayed on Easter cards—but an Empty Tomb.

St. Matthew, who alone gives us the account of the soldiers, is definite about this. He tells us they saw the angel who rolled back the stone and sat upon it. He does not say they saw the Risen Christ. Our Lord was no longer there. He did not have to wait for the stone to be removed before He could emerge from the tomb. We know that His Risen Body passed through the graveclothes without disturbing them. That is the point of St. John's careful description of the way they were found, "the napkin, that was about his head, not lying with the linen clothes, but wrapped together in a place by itself." The napkin lay collapsed where His head had been, above the linen cloth which had encased His body. Once He had passed through the graveclothes, there is no reason why He should not have proceeded at once to pass out of the tomb itself, unseen by the guard on watch.

On the other hand, there is a good reason why they should not have been permitted to see the Risen Christ. Our Lord appeared only to His disciples, to those who exercised a measure of faith. The soldiers, representatives of the indifferent or hostile world, were in no condition to experience the Resurrection. What they saw was the Empty Tomb. That was God's answer to man's plots and schemes to eliminate Him. In order to preserve their selfish interests, His enemies had crucified and buried Him. God flung open the door of the sepulchre and laid bare the fact that their devices had failed, their precautions had been in vain. God had escaped.

To the unbelieving world, the revelation had to be negative. God does not forcibly intervene in human affairs in order to thrust Himself upon man. Rather, He lets men see the emptiness and futility of their efforts to dispose of Him, to get along without Him. He warns them that they are on the wrong track and invites them to "repent in dust and ashes." He bids them return unto the Lord; but He does not compel them to heed Him.

God created man to love Him. Love is the free and willing gift of oneself to another. Hence man had to be given free will in order to be capable of love. He must exercise that love, that free will, in the very act by which he finds God. "We walk by faith, not by sight." God does not force Himself on our attention. Verily He is a God that hideth Himself. He reveals Himself, to be sure, but not in so overpowering a way as to prevent us from ignoring and denying Him. He gives us faith, the power to know Him.

But we must, of our own free will and effort, inspired, of course, by grace, co-operate with that virtue of faith, if it is to produce its intended effect. "Seek, and ye shall find." God wants our love. Hence, He must ask us to reach out in response to Him, however feebly, before He can take us up in His arms and clasp us to His heart.

In order that our choice of God may be a free, and, therefore, a loving act, He gives us the power to reject Him. We can, if we will, build for ourselves a world in which God is left out. Such a world is doomed ultimately to destroy itself. God loves us too much to allow us to proceed to our self-destruction without warning. Therefore, He first confronts us with the Empty Tomb to show us the futility of our attempts to eliminate Him.

The world in our own time has had just that experience. The last five centuries may be considered as a single epoch during which a new civilization has been built up in the western world. The process has been paced by the advance of science, in the widest sense of that word, knowledge about the universe and man. Success in that sphere has been phenomenal, and the practical application of that knowledge has revolutionized our way of life. The fundamental motives and ideals have been essentially good, the pursuit of truth, the betterment of living conditions, the spread of education, the establishment of justice, liberty, and peace. On the whole, there has been some progress toward the attainment of them.

But, as always, our old enemy pride has corrupted the process. The initial successes went to our heads. We have grown increasingly confident of our capacity to solve our problems by and for ourselves. Since our greatest progress has been in the area of material well-being, the desire to be self-sufficient has led us to define the good life more in terms of the things of this world, which we might hope to provide for ourselves, rather than in terms of the more elusive things of the spirit. The ill-informed opposition of conservative Churchmen at certain stages of the development convinced some of the pioneers that the Church is a center of reaction and obstruction. All this has fostered a tendency toward secularization. The cleavage between Church and State has, in several of the most "progressive" countries, become almost complete. The regulation of economic conditions, education, marriage, amusements, and works of mercy has been placed under the supervision of the State, the standards of which ultimately are human convenience and expediency.

Thus the modern world has gradually eliminated God. For secularism is essentially anti-religious. This fact is hidden from our eyes as long as the State is, on the whole, striving to achieve ideals it inherited from Christianity—liberty, equality, brotherhood. Yet, even in the most enlightened and morally respectable modern States, the discerning observer can see the anti-religious trend. Religion is looked upon more and more as an extra, which can be indulged in if one feels inclined, but is in no way necessary to the real business of life. The children in a secularized school are presented with what claims to be a satisfactory picture of the universe, from which God is either omitted entirely or only occasionally referred to in the vaguest and most platitudinous terms. Is it any wonder if some of them conclude that religion is an outworn superstition which should be discarded as soon as possible in the name of progress?

In the totalitarian State, secularism is finally unmasked. Hitler's New Order was a logical conclusion of the secular trend. If man, by increased knowledge and his own organization of society, without reference to or help from God, is able to produce Utopia, then it behooves man to be as efficient as possible about it. Let the State take complete control of the economic process, of education, and of family life. Let the whole be organized so as to produce the maximum material benefits in this life, since if there is any life after death, it is beyond human control and hence need not be taken into account. Let nothing, no matter how true or beautiful it may be, stand in the way of the most efficient functioning of the State. Let the scientist develop a master race by the same processes of selective breeding and elimination of the unfit as he would use in producing high-grade cattle. And let the master rule the world.

The master race appeared and men who had not lost all sense of divine values united to destroy it. In the process, our civilization, which had been so laboriously built up, and which contains so much that is high and noble, was plunged into war. The cost and sacrifices were enormous. For a while, it was doubtful whether our civilization would survive at all. By the grace and mercy of God, that danger was averted. We have another chance. But if we are to make the most of it, we must never forget the significance of WWII. The rise of totalitarianism was not the end of our civilization. It was a terrible warning that we have been moving along the wrong road. It was the Empty Tomb.

Does the analogy seem far-fetched? The Empty Tomb on Easter morning revealed the failure of the world's best efforts to preserve the Mosaic Law, the Jewish nation, and the *Pax Romana* by a process that eliminated God. God had reasserted Himself. The very presence of the guard on watch proved to the world that the body had been removed by no human agency. "This Jesus hath God raised up." God removed Himself and opened the tomb that they might see the emptiness and futility of their plots and schemes against Him.

In the totalitarian State, God, who had been progressively eliminated by the modern world's best efforts to achieve liberty, equality, brotherhood, prosperity, and peace, removed Himself entirely. He let men carry secularism to its logical and most successful conclusion, and thereby revealed that a State that finally crucifies and buries God is devoid of all good—is, in fact, an Empty Tomb.

Has the world heeded this final warning? It did not in our Lord's day. After the first shock of terror and confusion, it recomposed itself. It did not repent and return to God when faced with the Empty Tomb. Instead, the authorities produced a plausible explanation. "His disciples came by night, and stole him away while we slept." They knew it was false; but the world would accept it, for the action attributed to the disciples was just the kind of thing the world would do. Thus they carried on in the same old way, "the way that leadeth to destruction."

The good which they had tried to achieve and preserve by their own efforts without the help of God crumbled into dust in their final collapse. The Holy City and the glorious Temple were razed to the ground. The Chosen

People were scattered as homeless wanderers to the ends of the earth. The Mosaic Law which was to lead them to Christ became a heavy curtain blinding their eyes to their Messiah unto this day. The Roman Empire, decayed by dry-rot within, crumbled to ruin at the touch of the invading barbarians.

Not that these values were lost forever. The selfishness which had entwined itself about them was purged and cleansed away by the fire of destruction. The spiritual values of Judaism, however, were preserved and transmitted through the faithful remnant to the new Israel which is the Church. A temple not made with hands, eternal in the heavens, was substituted for that of Herod's building. The earthly Jerusalem, which was "in bondage with her children," was replaced by the "Jerusalem which is above," wherein "the Blessed have their dwelling-place and their rest forever and ever."

Still it was not God's will that the ancient expression of these values should be destroyed. Our Lord said, "Think not that I am come to destroy the Law, or the prophets: I am not come to destroy, but to fulfil." He had no quarrel with the benefits which came from membership in the Roman Empire. "Render unto Caesar the things which are Caesar's." When He contemplated the destruction which Jerusalem was about to bring on herself, He wept over the Holy City, "Jerusalem, Jerusalem . . . how often would I have gathered thy children together, as a hen doth gather her brood under her wings, and ye would not! . . . If thou hadst known, even thou, at least in this thy day, the things which belong unto thy peace! but now they are hid from thine eyes"—hid because of the selfish blindness of the people which had perverted the good things of God to their own ends and, therefore, involved them in their own destruction.

God does not want the noble ideals and worthy enterprises of the past five centuries to be buried in the night of new dark ages. Yet if we persist in depending on our own efforts to achieve them, and by that process exclude God from the major portions of our lives as individuals and as a society, then we shall involve them in our self-destruction. The rise of totalitarianism has shown us the end toward which secularism is inevitably moving. If, by continuing to pursue that policy, we cause totalitarianism to rise again, have we any assurance that the next time it will not engulf us?

We may well have had our last warning. Now that the dust of war has begun to settle, the question we should be asking ourselves is, have we heeded it? Are we seeking to know the things which belong unto our peace, the things of God? Or have we simply given a plausible explanation of the failure of our pre-war efforts to ward off totalitarianism and conflict? It stole upon us by night while we slept. A little more watchfulness, a little more skill in our human arrangements and devices, and we shall create the perfect world. Have we gone right back to the same old way, the way that leadeth to destruction?

Each of us must answer these questions first of all for himself. The world's decision depends more than we think on you and me. Ten righteous men would have saved Sodom from destruction. If enough of us choose the things of God, our civilization may yet be saved. If not, though it will be destroyed, those who have chosen God will be the remnant through which He will pass on the light to the new age that will be born. The choice is there for each of us to make. We have to make it whether we will or no. Not to choose God is to drift along with the world which rejects Him. We must either deny or worship the Risen Christ. The one thing we cannot do is to be neutral when we are faced with the Empty Tomb.

III

The Disciple Whom Jesus Loved

And when the sabbath was past, Mary Magdalene, and Mary the mother of James, and Salome, had bought sweet spices, that they might come and anoint him. And very early in the morning the first day of the week, they came unto the sepulchre at the rising of the sun. And they said among themselves, Who shall roll us away the stone from the door of the sepulchre? And when they looked, they saw that the stone was rolled away: for it was very great. And entering into the sepulchre, they saw a young man sitting on the right side, clothed in a long white garment; and they were affrighted. And he saith unto them, Be not affrighted: Ye seek Jesus of Nazareth, which was crucified: he is risen; he is not here: behold the place where they laid him. But go your way, tell his disciples and Peter that he goeth before you into Galilee: there shall ye see him, as he said unto you. And they went out quickly, and fled from the sepulchre; for they trembled and were amazed: neither said they any thing to any man; for they were afraid.

ST. MARK 16:1-8.

The first day of the week cometh Mary Magdalene early, when it was yet dark, unto the sepulchre, and seeth the stone taken away from the sepulchre. Then she runneth, and cometh to Simon Peter, and to the other disciple, whom Jesus loved, and saith unto them, They have taken away the Lord out of the sepulchre, and we know not where they have laid him. Peter therefore went forth, and that other disciple, and came to the sepulchre. So they ran both together: and the other disciple did outrun Peter, and came first to the sepulchre. And he stooping down, and looking in, saw the linen clothes lying; yet went he not in. Then cometh Simon Peter following him, and went into the sepulchre, and seeth the linen clothes lie, and the napkin, that was about his head, not lying with the linen clothes, but wrapped together in a place by itself. Then went in also that other disciple, which came first to the sepulchre, and he saw, and believed. For as yet they knew not the scripture, that he must rise again from the dead.

ST. JOHN 20:1-9.

The followers of our Lord also were confronted with the Empty Tomb. Very early on Sunday morning, a party of women set out from Jerusalem to visit the sepulchre. We are given the names of four of them: Mary Magdalene; Mary, the wife of Cleophas and mother of James and Joses; Salome, thought to be the wife of Zebedee and mother of James and John; and Joanna, wife of Chuza, Herod's steward. St. Luke suggests that there were others as well. They had bought spices the evening before, and were going to finish the anointing of the body, which they knew had been hurried and incomplete.

The two Marys had witnessed the interment. Joseph of Arimathea, a wealthy member of the Sanhedrin, had asked and obtained from Pilate permission to bury our Lord's body in his tomb on good Friday. Assisted by Nicodemus, a fellow-member of the Sanhedrin, and also, presumably, by a band of servants, Joseph had taken the body down from the cross, wrapped it in linen, and laid it in the sepulchre. The first three Gospels all seem to imply that Mary Magdalene and the other Mary had no share in the proceedings. This is understandable, since, as humble peasant women, they would have hesitated to intervene in

a matter which was being directed by two of the chief
men of Israel. They merely watched at a distance and saw
where the body was laid.

Naturally, the holy women desired to minister in person
to their Master's body and to complete with their own
hands what had been done hastily by others. Yet they knew
that it was dangerous to visit the tomb of One who had
been put to death for insurrection. The authorities would
tolerate no continuance of the movement He had started.
They already were furious with Joseph of Arimathea for
giving Him a decent burial.

The women hoped to circumvent this difficulty by starting early in the morning. They, of course, were unaware
that a guard had been set. For this was done on Saturday,
on which day they had not visited the tomb. But there was
another difficulty which they knew they must face. As
they hurried on in the grey light of early dawn, they
discussed it among themselves. "Who shall roll us away
the stone from the door of the sepulchre?"

The stone must have been very great if four or more
peasant women, accustomed as they were to heavy labor in
the house and field, feared they could not move it. It is the
measure of their determination to render their final service
to their dead Master that they set out to perform it knowing this obstacle lay across their path. Neither fear nor
difficulty could restrain the ardor of their love. God, they
intuitively felt, would find a way, if they on their part
made the attempt. It was the thing to do and they set out
to do it.

On entering the garden, they discovered that the anticipated difficulty had been removed. The stone was rolled

away from the sepulchre. But this filled them more with dismay than with relief. Hastening across the intervening space, they peered breathlessly into the semidarkness. Their worst fears were realized. Transfixed with grief, they dropped the now useless spices on the ground. The tomb was empty.

We must make an effort of imagination to enter into their experience at that moment. To us, the Empty Tomb means the Resurrection, so much so that the Gospels appointed by the Church to be read on Easter Day never carry us beyond the visit to the sepulchre. For Christians, that is enough. We know the tomb was empty because Christ had risen from the dead. Its very emptiness starts us shouting, "Alleluia!" To the holy women, it brought no such message of joy. "For as yet they knew not the scripture, that He must rise again from the dead." To them, it was the ultimate horror—a robbed grave.

Even that poor broken body which had been taken down from the cross had not been allowed to rest in the tomb. It was the culminating desecration. The last object on which they might have lavished their heart-broken ministrations had been taken from them. As thoughts such as these filled their minds, their cup of sorrow overflowed in a grief "too deep for tears."

After a moment of frozen stupor, one of the women broke from the group and rushed from the garden. This would seem to be the only way to reconcile the discrepancy in our accounts of the episode.[1] For in the first three Gospels, the discovery of the Empty Tomb is followed at once

---

[1] Dorothy Sayers works this scene out dramatically in *The Man Born to Be King*.

by the appearance of the angel (St. Luke says two angels) with the message that Christ is risen. Yet the Fourth Gospel asserts definitely that Mary Magdalene alone brought word of the Empty Tomb to Peter and John, and that she made no mention of any angelic message. Since she would hardly have failed to speak of this had she heard it, we are forced to conclude that she left before the angel was seen.

Two little phrases in the variant accounts point in the same direction. Both St. Mark and St. Luke state explicitly that it was after the women had entered "into the sepulchre" that the angel was discovered. St. John, on the other hand, says, "Mary Magdalene . . . seeth the stone taken away from the sepulchre. Then she runneth, and cometh to Simon Peter." One glimpse into the Empty Tomb is enough to start the impetuous Magdalene off for the disciples. It is characteristic of St. John thus to correct the earlier accounts without specifically contradicting them.

After Mary Magdalene left, the other women recovered sufficiently from their initial shock to investigate further. Then they saw the angel and heard his message: "Ye seek Jesus of Nazareth, which was crucified: he is risen; he is not here: behold the place where they laid him. But go your way, tell his disciples and Peter that he goeth before you into Galilee: there shall ye see him, as he said unto you."

Encouraging as the angel's words sound to us, who know the full truth of the Resurrection, they could hardly have been so to the holy women. The vision of an angel was in itself a terrifying experience. His message, so completely unexpected, must have been almost unintelligible to them. They could not absorb or understand its meaning. Probably, if it conveyed anything to them at all, it gave them a vague and uneasy impression that somehow the Lord was alive. Far from removing the terror which the discovery of the Empty Tomb had impressed upon them, it greatly increased it. They fled from the sepulchre in amazement and fear.

Meanwhile, Mary Magdalene reached Peter and John. "They have taken away the Lord out of the sepulchre, and we know not where they have laid him." At once the disciples set out for the garden, with Mary Magdalene following them. Apparently, taking a slightly different route through the crooked little streets of the city, they missed the party of women who were returning. They reached the sepulchre and found it as Mary Magdalene had described it. No angel appeared. Without any mitigation, they were made to face the Empty Tomb.

Let us pause to ask why our Lord permitted His best-loved friends to undergo this fearful and desolating experience. They had suffered so much already in His crucifixion and death. Why did He not spare them the added horror of thinking that His body had been stolen from the tomb? At first thought, it would seem as if He could have done so very easily. Could He not have appeared to the holy women before they reached the sepulchre? Could He not have appeared to Peter and John while they sat talking in the house?

The answer to these questions, humanly speaking, is "No." Or, to put it more accurately, though He could have appeared to them, it is very doubtful whether He could have convinced them that He had risen from the dead. As long as they were certain in their minds that His body lay in the sepulchre without the walls of the city, would they ever have believed that they were experiencing more than a vision of a ghost? We shall see, when we come to the Appearance in the Upper Room, to what lengths our Lord had to go to convince them of the reality of His Risen Body, even after they knew that the tomb was empty. Could He have done so before that fact had been driven home?

This situation reminds us of one of the fundamental principles of the spiritual life. Not only do men's attempts to build for themselves a world that leaves out God have to be rebuked by the Empty Tomb. Their best efforts to find and serve Him end in the same experience. But its purpose is different. For those who rebel against God, the revelation of the futility of their plots and schemes is a warning, calling them to repentance. For those who are seeking God, the Empty Tomb is a purgation preparing them for a greater revelation than they had expected.

Blatant selfishness is not the only barrier which keeps us from God. Our own highest thoughts about Him, our own sincerest efforts to serve Him can also be obstacles, precisely because they are our own. We do not find God, serve God, love God in our own strength. We are found by Him, used by Him; "we love him, because he first loved us." We are to lose ourselves in God. When we do that, we find ourselves in Him.

The truth is that God is too big for our minds. Yet we are perpetually trying to whittle Him down and fit Him in. He comes to us and we respond to Him. Thereby, we gain some insight into His truth, His beauty, and His love. Since He can give us only what we are capable of receiving, and our capacity is so small, it is a very partial revelation. We take it, however, and proceed at once to treat it as the fulness of truth. We erect it into an all-embracing dogma and refuse to believe not only that which contradicts it, but also anything that might supplement it. On the basis of this ultimate truth which we suppose we possess, we map out the rest of our lives and ask no more of God than that He speed us on our way. Hence, the use we make of the revelation does not permit it to have its intended effect of increasing our capacity for God. Instead, we clutter up our souls with a host of inferences and plans of our own devising.

When God wills to give us a further revelation of Himself, there is no room in our hearts to receive it. God must first sweep away those cherished idols which our hands have fashioned. The fact that we have made them with the best intentions of serving God, and have molded them out of the revelation God gave us, renders their destruction all the more painful to us. It seems as though all the truth, all the beauty, all the love, yes, as though God Himself, had gone out of our lives. But this is, nonetheless, the necessary prelude to a deeper comprehension of His love.

By the morning of the third day, our Lord's followers were beginning to adjust themselves to the fact of the Crucifixion. They were taking up their lives again. We have seen the holy women set out for the tomb to do honor to Christ's memory by finishing the ministrations to His dead body. Peter and John, no doubt, were discussing how they would carry on now that He was no longer with them. They would retire to Galilee where they would be safe from the authorities who had crucified Him. They would collect his words and acts into a book and circulate it privately. In time, it would find its place in the Scriptures with the Books of Isaiah, Jeremiah, and Ezekiel. Along such lines as these, perhaps, they were mapping out the future on the basis of a partial revelation which they mistakenly thought was completed on Calvary. There was no room in their plans for the Resurrection.

Had our Lord appeared to them without first destroying their conviction that He was dead and buried, what would they have thought? They would have been grateful for the Vision which refreshed their memory of His dear features. They might even have felt an increased assurance that in some vague sense He was alive, far away, awaiting the Resurrection at the last day. Their zeal to serve Him according to their own lights would have been increased.

Their own lights were not enough. They hid from their eyes the true Light which is Christ. Therefore, their lights were extinguished in the darkness of the Empty Tomb.

Darkness, yes, but Francis Thompson points to its true significance:

> Is my gloom, after all,
> Shade of His hand, outstretched caressingly?

It was the purifying darkness which emptied them of self that they might be filled with God. It was the divine darkness, the over-shadowing of God's approaching love. It was the dazzled darkness of excess of light.

So consistently does this experience repeat itself as one follows the way of love that some have come to recognize the descent of darkness itself as the herald of the dawn. When they find their hearts failing them for fear, they look up and lift up their heads; for they know that their redemption draweth nigh.

There was one who did that in the Empty Tomb. He was John, the disciple whom Jesus loved. As has often been pointed out, John's title did not mean that our Lord preferred John to the others. The Master offered the fulness of His perfect human love equally to all the Twelve, to Judas as much as to the rest. But, whereas Judas increasingly rejected it, and the others accepted it hesitantly and sparingly, John allowed his heart to be opened the widest to receive it. The process, however, even for him, had been slow and painful. He did not start as the Beloved Disciple. He started as one of the "sons of thunder." There was in him an element of hot-headed impetuosity of which he had to be emptied before he could learn the art of loving and of being loved. The cleansing and opening of his heart gave him many opportunities to discover that the increase of the capacity for love is preceded by an experience of purifying darkness.

St. Luke records for us one instance of how John's hot-headedness was rebuked. Our Lord and His followers were setting out on the last journey through Samaria. The disciples were already becoming confused as to what His plans were. He Himself, on the other hand, displayed more certainty and determination than ever. "He stedfastly set his face to go to Jerusalem."

As evening approached, He sent some of the party ahead to arrange for lodging in the next village. The Samaritans there refused to entertain a group bound for the Holy City. When James and John heard this, anger welled up in them. It was an insult to the Messiah. Remembering how Elijah had called down fire from heaven on those sent to arrest him, the sons of thunder asked permission to treat the inhospitable villagers in the same way. Whereupon the Lord "turned and rebuked them"— there is an inescapable note of sharpness in those verbs. "Ye know not what manner of spirit ye are of. For the Son of man is not come to destroy men's lives, but to save them."

Those words must have stung John like a slap in the face. This episode occurred shortly after the Transfiguration, when Peter and James and John had seen something of the Lord's glory shining through His human nature. Both the joy and the intimacy of that night on the mountain top gave John a sense of having penetrated into the mystery of Jesus. He felt he understood it all. Jesus was the heavenly Messiah about to proclaim His Kingdom. Moses and Elijah courted and attended Him. His power, clearly greater than theirs, was about to be revealed. Seizing on this one aspect of the truth, John allowed it so to dominate his mind that when an opportunity came to use the power as Elijah had done, he was quick to suggest it.

With the rebuke came the realization that he was all wrong. The Master, whom he so loved and whose honor he had sought to defend, was pained and offended. John felt all drained out, empty, bewildered, hurt. Just as he thought he was beginning to see light, everything went black. His most cherished hopes and dreams fell in ruins at his feet.

He accepted the darkness, however, and learned its lesson. He let our Lord give him thereby a deeper insight into His true spirit. John's mistaken concept of an avenging messiah having been shattered, he was able to comprehend, at least dimly, that his Master was to enter His Kingdom by being the Suffering Servant of whom Isaiah had spoken. He was not to smite down His enemies. Rather, He Himself was to be despised and rejected of men; He was to be wounded for our transgressions and bruised for our iniquities; He was to be taken from prison and from judgment, and brought as a lamb to the slaughter. The Lord was to lay on Him the iniquity of us all, and by His stripes we were to be healed.

As a result of this insight, John alone among the Twelve was able to attend our Lord faithfully during His Passion and minister to Him his sympathy and comfort. How rapidly his love grew! In Samaria, he would not brook the discourtesy shown Christ by the villagers. His love of the Master could reach no higher than a demand for vengeance. In Jerusalem, he saw his Master arrested, condemned, mocked, scourged, crucified. This was only a few days after the Samaritan episode. Yet his love had now reached the stature that he was able to perceive that, in surrendering Himself, Christ was fulfilling the Father's Will. John trusted Jesus to know what was the right course. He neither sought to restrain Him from it, nor protested against it. Our Lord's patience in bearing His sufferings was matched by John's patience in watching Him bear them. Anyone who has ever seen a loved one suffer and been unable to prevent or alleviate the pain knows something of what it cost John to attend Christ's cross in Christ's own loving spirit of forgiving His enemies. Such was the capacity for love which that stinging rebuke opened in John's heart.

This is but one incident, which happens to be recorded for us, among the many by which our Lord transformed the son of thunder into the Beloved Disciple. John must often have passed through darkness into a clearer comprehension and experience of love. He had learned the rhythm of the spiritual life. When the darkness of the Empty Tomb fell upon him, he was able to understand it.

At first, it was very dark. Mary Magdalene's report that the body had been stolen filled John with dismay. In his eagerness to prove that it was not so, he outstripped Peter to the tomb. But the facts confirmed the report. Save for the linen clothes, the sepulchre was empty. Sick at heart, John went not in.

Peter did. From John's own account, it seems that Peter first discovered the peculiar arrangement of the shroud and called John's attention to it. Peter apparently could make nothing of it.

But John was wrestling with the darkness. Was this, like its predecessors, a sign of approaching light? Had he once more underestimated the loving-kindness of the Lord? He entered the tomb looking for grounds of faith and hope. Did the grave-clothes supply them? They had never been unwrapped. They still bore in their collapsed state the impress of the body they had contained. How could the body have been removed without disturbing them?

"Lazarus, come forth. . . . I am the Resurrection and the Life. . . . Destroy this temple, and in three days I will raise it up. . . . They shall scourge him, and put him to death: and the third day he shall rise again." And John "saw and believed."

John, the Beloved Disciple, the one among the Twelve who was most faithful in following the way of love, had a unique privilege. He was called to share with the others the apostolic vocation of seeing the Risen Christ and of bearing witness to the Resurrection. With this vocation, he alone succeeded in combining the seemingly contradictory blessing of those who have not seen and yet have believed. For before he saw the Risen Christ he saw the Empty Tomb and believed.

IV

The Faithful Follower

Mary stood without at the sepulchre weeping: and as she wept, she stooped down, and looked into the sepulchre, and seeth two angels in white sitting, the one at the head, and the other at the feet, where the body of Jesus had lain. And they say unto her, Woman, why weepest thou? She saith unto them, Because they have taken away my Lord, and I know not where they have laid him. And when she had thus said, she turned herself back, and saw Jesus standing, and knew not that it was Jesus. Jesus saith unto her, Woman, why weepest thou? whom seekest thou? She, supposing him to be the gardener, saith unto him, Sir, if thou have borne him hence, tell me where thou hast laid him, and I will take him away. Jesus saith unto her, Mary. She turned herself, and saith unto him, Rabboni; which is to say, Master. Jesus saith unto her, Touch me not; for I am not yet ascended to my Father: but go to my brethren, and say unto them, I ascend unto my Father, and your Father; and to my God, and your God. Mary Magdalene came and told the disciples that she had seen the Lord, and that he had spoken these things unto her.

ST. JOHN 20:11-18.

If we make the traditional identification of Mary Magdalene with the woman "which was a sinner" and with Mary of Bethany, the sister of Lazarus and Martha, we get a full-length portrait of Christian vocation. So consistent is her character and so clearly can we trace in her the steps by which a soul is drawn into union with Christ, that this in itself is evidence for the validity of the tradition.

Mary Magdalene, then, enters the Gospel narrative as a sinner. No indication is given as to the nature of her sins. The tendency has been to give the word the meaning it would have in ordinary parlance and to assume that she was a harlot. In favor of this interpretation, there is the vehemence of her act of penitence—bursting in on our Lord while He sat at dinner in a rich man's house and falling in tears at His feet. Psychologically, this action is more readily explained if she had gross and shameful sins on her conscience.

There is, however, another possible meaning of the word in its original setting. The scene of Mary's penitence was the house of Simon the Pharisee, and the purpose of the descriptive epithet is to explain Simon's antipathy to her. Now, among the Pharisees, the word *sinner* had a technical significance. It was used to designate anyone who kept the Jewish Law with less than pharisaic strictness. Hence, it may be that Mary Magdalene was simply one of what today would be called the emancipated set, who sit lightly to religious obligations when they are in conflict with carefree *camaraderie* and the pursuit of pleasure.

The latter possibility is worth noting because we have far too strong a tendency to equate sin with crime, or at least with serious acts of wrongdoing. Sins of word, thought, and omission are almost entirely overlooked. This is a false and unfair standard which fails to take into account the part that temperament, environment, and opportunity play in determining the form in which temptations come to us. As these are largely beyond the control of the individual, they must be discounted in judging his guilt. "Arsenic and Old Lace" to the contrary notwithstanding, respectable old ladies are not often tempted to commit murder. They may, however, express a murderous degree of hatred of their neighbors and rejection of God by indulging in back-fence gossip.

Our Lord made it clear that God does discount the form in which temptation comes. In the Sermon on the Mount He said that an angry insult, "Thou fool," is the equivalent of murder, and that he who "looketh on a woman to lust after her hath committed adultery with her already in his heart." The consent of the will to temptation is what constitutes sin. The amount of rejection of God's love which that consent entails determines its seriousness. The form in which the temptation comes and the consequent damage to society which results from yielding to it are not relevant in assessing an individual's guilt in so far as they are determined by factors beyond his control.

We need not know, therefore, what acts of sin Mary Magdalene had committed. The essential nature of her sin is clear. She had lived for herself. Her outstanding characteristic was a great capacity for love, which later was to enable her to enter, through contemplation, into the closest intimacy with God. Before her conversion, she tried to express and satisfy this desire for union with others, not by giving herself generously to them and through them to God, but by seeking to possess them for herself apart from God. She sought by her personal attractiveness to win and bind people to herself, disregarding God's will when to do so would gain their praise and favor, and she hoped to find lasting happiness in her relationships with them. To this end, she may or she may not have played the harlot with men. That makes relatively little difference. What is important is that, in prostituting her capacity for love into a quest for selfish pleasure, she played the harlot from her God.

She did not find the happiness she craved. Then, one day, she met Reality Incarnate in Christ Jesus. Deep in her heart was born a love that made all her former selfish loves seem cheap and paltry. More than that, she felt herself soiled and polluted by them. Could she, sinner that she was, dare to hope that her love would be acceptable to Him who was spotlessly pure?

There followed a period of hesitation and indecision. But her yearning love finally gained control. Once it had, her impetuosity would brook no delay. She must go to Him immediately, regardless of what it cost. Having determined to throw herself on His mercy, she made no effort to spare herself a public humiliation. It was not easy to enter the house of Simon the Pharisee. For years, he had pointed the finger of condemnation and scorn at her. She and the smart set with which she traveled retaliated by calling him a pious fool. They were mortal enemies. Now she was ready to brave even his hostility in order to approach the Master in humble penitence. She welcomed the opportunity to make a total repudiation of her former life. She loved much.

In spite of her sins, her love was not spurned. The Master let her wash His feet with her tears and wipe them with the hairs of her head. Her penitence was accepted. She,

who had tried so hard to create for herself by her own
efforts a lasting happiness and security and had failed so
consistently, found it now in her act of utter, helpless
surrender. She learned the first lesson of love.

She also found a champion. She was not unaware of
Simon's unspoken contempt. In her new-born joy, she was
content to bear it. It was enough that the Master did not
send her away. But He sprang to her defense. "Simon, I
have somewhat to say unto thee." There followed that
stinging rebuke in which her humble penitence was con-
trasted with Simon's smug self-righteousness, her tearful
service with his condescending patronage. How her heart
leapt at those words, not with pride at the Master's praise,
but with the thrilling realization of what the way of
love was like. It was not to be the frigid righteousness, the
cramped scrupulosity of the Pharisee. It was to be a path
of adventure in which one dared to follow bold and generous impulses. It did not involve meticulous adherence
to a multiplicity of laws, but instead it beckoned one
on to the glorious liberty of complete self-abandonment
into the hands of God.

"Thy sins are forgiven. Thy faith hath saved thee: go
in peace." These words ushered Mary Magdalene into a
new life, one called, in the technical language of ascetic
theology, the illuminative way. She was to be led on from
her act of self-abasing penitence into the positive joys of
life with God. True conversion is never the end. It is the
starting point of a new beginning.

Mary Magdalene at once became one of the holy women
who followed our Lord and "ministered unto him of their
substance." Thus, she had the privilege of serving Him and

His disciples. She was not content, however, merely with service. Her love was too deep to allow her to substitute work for personal devotion. Her humility was too sincere for her to think that she could do anything for the Master commensurate with what He could do for her. She served Him, yes; but she also knew when to sit at His feet and hear His word.

She avoided the mistake her sister Martha made. Martha represents a type of so-called Christians, very common today, who are unwilling to make a genuine personal surrender to Christ. To escape this surrender they throw themselves into a frenzy of service. They are perpetually bustling about helping others, serving on committees, running charitable enterprises. Some of them retain membership in a Christian Church, but prayer occupies a small place in their lives, penitence is the vague admission that after all they do not pretend to be perfect, and worship is something they attend to set a good example. Others of them have frankly discarded the Church as an inefficient social agency and work entirely through secular organizations. But even the latter group, still more the former, consider themselves to be fine examples of how to love God and one's neighbor. They have the utmost scorn for those who are less absorbed in charitable activities than they are and brand as an ineffectual and self-centered piety any suggestion of the priority of prayer over service.

This last attitude is what unmasked Martha and revealed how selfish was her fundamental motivation. What, actually, was she trying to accomplish by all that activity in which she had been engaged ever since our Lord's arrival in her house? Everything was ready long before He came. The fussy straightening of the tableware, the slight readjustment of this and that, the repeated trips to the stove to check the cooking for the hundredth time, had these any real purpose except to draw attention and praise of herself? By her every act she was shouting to the Master, "See how much I am doing for you." He knew this too well to give her the praise she craved.

Martha did not love our Lord with personal devotion. She would not give herself to Him in penitence and prayer. That cost more than she was willing to pay. She served Him in order to avoid having to make the sacrifice which love involves. When the Master did not accept her substitute and commend her as she expected, anger filled her heart. Mary, who, by doing nothing, seemed to be winning His love, was an obvious target for her wrath. She would drag Mary down to her level of bustling, unsurrendered service. "Lord, dost thou not care that my sister hath left me to serve alone? bid her therefore that she help me."

Our Lord's answer revealed Martha to herself. "Martha, Martha, thou art careful and troubled about many things: but one thing is needful: and Mary hath chosen that good part, which shall not be taken away from her." Martha's true conversion, no doubt, dates from this episode. She, like her sister, is counted among the Church's saints. But her vocation remained different from Mary's. Martha represents the active life. She continued to be occupied in many things. She still performed them carefully, but she was less troubled, for she was no longer striving to make an impression. She learned the necessity of prayer and penitence as the basis of the active life. Above all, she made her service an expression of genuine self-giving, of personal devotion. Her work itself became a form of prayer. Many souls are called to the active life, the service of God and of God in man, in the humble round of daily tasks. It is a real vocation, and by following it selflessly they also may scale the spiritual heights.

Mary, on the other hand, was called to spend more time in contemplation. She had chosen the good part which was not taken away from her. She had her work to do. Before the Master's arrival, she had been as busy as Martha getting things prepared. But when He came, she felt called to leave the lesser things in order to sit at His feet and hear His word. It is significant that, because she was faithful to this vocation, she caused Martha to find hers. The witness of the contemplative life is necessary to the active life, to remind those called to the latter that service is not an end in itself, nor is its aim chiefly the well-being of man. Like prayer, it must be the means of unlimited self-oblation to God.

The Master confirmed Mary in her vocation to the contemplative life and she continued to run gaily along the path of love throughout our Lord's public ministry. Only once, and then but briefly, did a shadow fall across her path. Lazarus, her brother, died and Jesus was far away. He had ignored her frantic message asking for His aid. Mary, as well as Martha, could not help rebuking Him when He came, "Lord, if thou hadst been here, my brother had not died." Yet the shadow was but the prelude to the brighter light; the truth of the Resurrection was foreshadowed in the raising of Lazarus from the tomb.

Mary's devotion and service found its climax in worship.

Her intuition, made sensitive by love, told her that Jesus deserved the highest reverence and honor. Was He not the Messiah, the Anointed One? Her generosity prompted her to make Him as fitting an offering as she could. The box of ointment was a costly gift. (Three hundred pence, for which Judas estimated it could have been sold, would be about a year's wage of a workman, if we take the "penny a day," mentioned in the parable of the laborers in the vineyard, as the current standard.) In the same attitude of humble reverence in which she had approached Him as a penitent, she now brought her gift of worship. She anointed His feet and wiped them with the hairs of her head. Then, breaking the box, she poured the last drops on His head, "and the house was filled with the odor of the ointment." Her offering was a holocaust, entirely devoted to Him.

Judas complained of the waste. The ointment should have been sold and the money given to the poor. But again our Lord approved Mary's action. "The poor always ye have with you; but me ye have not always." True worship never conflicts with charity to the poor. He who gives himself generously to the adoration of God, which is the essence of worship, will be lifted thereby into a spirit of love which sends him from the altar the more determined to relieve those in need. It is by joining with our brethren in the effort to love God with all our hearts and minds and souls that we get the incentive and the power to love our neighbor as ourself.

Worship is our first duty and our highest privilege. By rendering God our best in praise and thanksgiving we make a little response to the love He lavishes upon us.

We engage for a moment on earth in what will be our eternal joy in heaven. Mary Magdalene manifested a true sense of spiritual values when she sacrificed her most treasured possession to give our Lord the honor she believed to be His due. He accepted her tribute. This was significant. It involved a public admission that He was the Messiah. He prefaced His commendation of her action with the words, "Against the day of my burying hath she kept this." But this somber prophecy passed unnoticed at the time by all except Judas. What impressed others was His willingness to receive the anointing with all its implications. It raised in their hearts the hope that He was about to proclaim and establish His Messianic Kingdom.

Subsequent events strengthened that hope. On Palm Sunday, He made His triumphal entry into Jerusalem. This was followed by the cleansing of the Temple, which rallied the common people to Him. For at least two days, He spoke boldly and openly to ever-increasing crowds, confounding all those sent by His enemies to entrap Him. Never had His popularity reached such a height. He could count on a huge following if He chose to raise the standard of revolt. When on Thursday, after a day of rest and retirement in Bethany, Jesus set out with the Twelve for the Holy City, it was clear to everyone that the hour of crisis was at hand. None felt it so keenly as Mary Magdalene. She stood at the summit of the illuminative way, expecting to pass at once into the glory of the Messianic Kingdom.

She was plunged instead into the "dark night of the soul." Sometime early on Friday morning, probably, word reached Bethany that Jesus had been arrested. At once, the holy

women set out to accompany His Mother to the cross.
They met Jesus on the way of sorrows and followed him
to Calvary. There Mary Magdalene watched Him who had
been the center and substance of her life for the past two
or three years, as He was put to a slow, shameful, and
agonizing death. She who had ministered to Him so often
could do so no more. She could not even press water to
those parched lips or wipe the sweat and blood from His
face. She could only fall before His cross and weep.

The hours of the Sabbath crawled by and, with the
dawn, she and the other women set out for the sepulchre
to give the final ministrations to His body. We have already
seen Mary Magdalene, reeling under the impact of the
Empty Tomb, dash off to inform Peter and John. She
followed them back. After they had completed their in-
vestigations and departed, she remained outside the sepulchre, weeping. Was it to this that her faithful following
of the Master had brought her? There she stood amid
the discarded spices, those eloquent symbols of frustrated
service. Was this the end—an Empty Tomb?

Mary could not tear herself away. Whither should she
go? Her faithfulness to duty had brought her there and
she had received no indication of what she was to do next.
She waited in the darkness and emptiness for God to act.

Even the appearance of the angels was no consolation
to her. She seems to have been strangely indifferent to
them. "Woman, why weepest thou?" "Because they have
taken away my Lord, and I know not where they have laid
him." She sought Jesus, just His poor, broken, dead body,
to be sure, but still His body, and no angels from heaven
could take its place. Jesus first, Jesus last, Jesus only was

the object of her love. She turned away from the angels, her grief unassuaged. This rejection of the sweetness of spiritual consolation as a substitute for the reality of God Himself was her final and supreme act of faithfulness. Through it she found Him whom her soul loved. So quietly and so naturally did He appear that she mistook Him for the gardener. Still absorbed in her quest, she said, "Sir, if thou have borne him hence, tell me where thou hast laid him, and I will take him away." "Mary." "Rabboni." And she threw herself at His feet.

At the feet of Jesus, there is where we always find her. She washed His feet with penitential tears. She sat at His feet and heard His word. She anointed His feet with the ointment. She knelt at the foot of the cross. Now she is the first to kiss the feet of the Risen Christ. Is this surprising? She had followed the call of Christ step by step without faltering. Nothing, not the humiliation of penitence, not the snare of conventional service, not the cost of sacrifice, not the suffering of Calvary, not the frustration of the Empty Tomb, not the angelic consolation, nothing could turn her from seeking Him. As in geometry, so in the spiritual life, a straight line is the shortest distance between two points. She who moved in a direct quest for Christ was inevitably the first to behold His risen glory.

This experience was for Mary Magdalene the culmination of the illuminative way. In it she was called to take yet another step and pass on into the unitive life. She was bidden to surrender that which had been so far the driving-power of her response to Christ. Her devotion, heretofore, had been expressed in an attachment to Him as He revealed Himself through His human body. Her love had taken the form of ministrations to Him in that body. Her refusal to leave the spot where last His body had been laid kept her faithful at the sepulchre until He manifested Himself to her in that body now risen from the grave. Soon, however, that body would no longer be visibly present on earth. So, as He revealed Himself to Mary in that body, our Lord called her to a more spiritual and therefore more enduring relationship with Him. "Touch me not," or as some prefer to translate it, "Do not keep clinging to me." Mary was to rise up now to the unitive life in which, no longer dependent on occasional visible manifestations of Christ, she was to abide in constant companionship with Him through sacraments and contemplation.

Here, then, is a full-length picture of the path of Christian vocation. It began in humble and costly penitence, a conversion from the way of sin to the life in Christ. It led her on through prayer and service until she was able to make more and more generous offerings of herself. Once devotion to Christ had taken unshakable root in her soul, she underwent the final purgation in which every vestige of self-love and self-dependence was burned away. She suffered the loss of all that she held dear, in order that she might have the opportunity to express her love and faithfulness to Christ for His sake alone, not for any benefit she received therefrom. Her faith and hope in Him was tested by her witnessing His apparent defeat and failure. Her love was tried by having to undergo the frustration of her final effort to minister to Him and by the fear that she had lost Him forever. Her desire for Him alone was proved by her rejection of spiritual consolation as a substitute for His presence. Having triumphantly passed these tests, she was rewarded by His Appearance, during which He lifted her up to the highest relationship of a soul with Christ in this life—the Unitive Way.

Many saints have followed Mary Magdalene along this path. They have shared with her the humiliation of the penitential life and the joys of the illuminative. They have been plunged into the self-emptying darkness of frustration, suffering, and the apparent loss of God. They have been tried by the experience of ecstasies which they have resisted as best they might. Although they have not enjoyed an Appearance of the Risen Christ—since that was not their vocation—yet their faithfulness through all the trials has been rewarded by an intimate spiritual contact with our Lord which they try to designate in our inadequate human speech by such terms as the "spiritual marriage of the soul with God," by which they have been lifted into the life of abiding union with Him.

This path lies open before us all. Only our lack of generosity in self-surrender holds us back from it. As He called Mary Magdalene, our Lord calls us step by step. If, as she did, we respond whole-heartedly to each call, we are drawn straight along the highroad that leads to union with God. Not that the road will look straight as we follow it. It did not look straight to her. It seemed full of inexplicable twists and turns; it mounted heights of exaltation and plunged into depths of grief; it appeared to terminate in the frustration of the Empty Tomb. Yet it was the path, and for her the only path, which led straight to the Heart of God. For each of us there is such a path at our feet. Please God we shall find and follow it. We shall, if we answer His calls as they come.

V

The Penitent

The Lord is risen indeed, and hath appeared to Simon.
                                        ST. LUKE 24:34.

*For I delivered unto you first of all that which I also received,
how that Christ died for our sins according to the scriptures;
and that he was buried, and that he rose again the third day
according to the scriptures: and that he was seen of Cephas,
then of the twelve.*
                              I CORINTHIANS 15:3-5.

Peter did not believe when he saw the Empty Tomb.
The possibility of the Resurrection never occurred to him.
He saw the evidence of the grave-clothes; indeed, he seems
to have called John's attention to it. But Peter was too absorbed in his own thoughts to consider the evidence objectively. To him the Empty Tomb was simply a robbed
grave and an added weight to his already unbearable load
of grief.

Peter had failed his Master. He had failed Him in terms
of what he felt, and felt rightly, was his strongest characteristic—his loyalty. Ever since that moment on the lake-
shore of Galilee when Peter was called to be a disciple,
he had tried to follow the Master with unswerving devotion. His initial surrender had been unconditional. Like
that of Mary Magdalene, it had involved a penitent reckon-

ing of his worthlessness. After the miraculous draught of fishes, Peter, sensing that in Jesus God was manifesting Himself to an extraordinary degree, threw himself at our Lord's feet. But even while, in oriental fashion, he seized Him about the knees, he cried, "Depart from me; for I am a sinful man, O Lord."

That honest self-appraisal and humble self-surrender made possible his call, "Follow me, and I will make you a fisher of men." Peter left all and followed Christ. He left his home, his trade, his wife, and, presumably, his children. He cast in his lot with that itinerant Preacher. He stuck by Him through good times and ill. His one desire was to learn the Master's mind and carry out His will. This single-hearted loyalty enabled him to become one of the inner circle of the Twelve and their chief spokesman. It gave him occasional flashes of insight, the climax of which was his inspired exclamation at Caesarea Philippi, "Thou are the Christ, the Son of the living God." Recognizing the potential power of that loyalty, our Lord was able to respond, "Thou art Peter, and upon this rock I will build my Church."

Peter, of course, had natural qualities of leadership. He was endowed with them by God in order that he might fulfil the vocation to which he was called. He had a burning yet practical zeal, an ability to make and carry out decisions, a strong personality which attracted and inspired others. But all these natural talents would not of themselves have made Peter the Prince of the Apostles. They had to be consecrated to our Lord before they could be used as the instrument of God's work in the world. Peter's unswerving loyalty was what made their consecration possible.

This will be seen more clearly if we contrast Peter with another of the Twelve who, though he is always portrayed in deep shadows, gives us the impression of being a man of outstanding natural endowments. Judas was not only a traitor. He was also one of the Twelve. Unless we are to maintain that our Lord chose Judas in order that the latter might damn himself by betraying his Master, a view violently inconsistent with the love of God and with the character of Jesus, we must assume that he had at first the same potentiality of becoming a saint as had the rest of the Twelve. The fact that he was appointed to keep the bag, that is, to handle the practical aspects of the common life of the Apostles, must mean that he had executive ability. Our Lord recognized his talents and was prepared to use them to the full.

Yet, in the end, Judas betrayed Him. Why? We cannot hope to determine his motives with any certainty from the scanty evidence which has come down to us. To attribute his fall to a sudden impulse of greed for thirty pieces of silver is clearly unsatisfactory. It fails to explain why he went to the chief priests in the first place and let them make the offer. The first three Gospels all make it clear that Judas took the initiative in going to the priests, and the first two associate his decision with the episode in which Mary Magdalene anointed our Lord as the Messiah and with His assertion that "she is come aforehand to anoint my body to the burying."

This tends to endorse what may be considered the most plausible explanation of Judas' treachery. Not only did he fail to understand the spiritual nature of Jesus' Messiahship and to see that our Lord had to suffer and die in order to accomplish His work of redemption. All the Apostles failed to grasp that. Judas, unlike the others, presumed to judge our Lord mistaken in His rejection of the vocation to be an earthly, warrior Messiah, in His refusal to establish His Kingdom by the use of force. Jesus, in his mind, was missing His opportunity when He did not use His popularity to organize a revolt against the Roman yoke and against the Jewish leaders who acquiesced in submitting to it. This reestablishment of Jewish independence was what Judas expected of the Messiah. When Jesus failed to strive for it, Judas concluded that He was an impostor who had better be repudiated and destroyed, especially if, by engineering that end, Judas could gain advantage for himself.

If this motivation be correct, it shows that Judas did not submit himself whole-heartedly into our Lord's hands to be guided and taught. He clung to his own criteria of what a Messiah should be and judged his Master in terms of them. When Jesus failed to measure up, that proved that Jesus was wrong. Judas would follow Him only in so far as Judas thought He was right. This deficiency in loyalty made Judas unteachable.

Peter also misjudged his Master. His mistake, however, sprang from an excess of loyal zeal. He would not tolerate any suggestion that there could be difficulties or failure in Jesus' path. When our Lord Himself, right after approving Peter's insight into His Messiahship, began to predict His Passion, Peter at once exclaimed, "Be it far from thee, Lord: this shall not be unto thee." Like Judas, Peter could not conceive of a messianic vocation except in terms of a swift and forceful triumph over His enemies. But since Peter's blindness rested not on intellectual pride but on a loyalty that would admit no possibility of the Master's defeat, it was curable. When our Lord, who had so recently commended him, now said to Peter, "Get thee behind me, Satan: thou art an offense unto me," Peter no doubt gasped with surprise, but he did not leap to the conclusion that he was right and Jesus was wrong. Though he was cut to the quick and utterly confused, he took the full blame upon himself and tried all the harder to understand the Master's purpose.

Loyalty was Peter's strong suit and he knew it. Therefore, our Lord's remarks to him at the Last Supper were disquieting. "Simon, Simon, behold, Satan hath desired to have you, that he may sift you as wheat: but I have prayed for thee, that thy faith fail not: and when thou art converted, strengthen thy brethren." Peter sensed a prediction of disloyalty in this and was quick to repudiate it. "Lord, I am ready to go with thee, both into prison, and to death." This boast shows that Peter had learned to accept the fact of our Lord's impending suffering which he had at first rejected at Caesarea Philippi. He believed the Master knew what He was doing and he was prepared to follow Him, whatever the cost. But was he? Jesus did not think so. "I tell thee, Peter, the cock shall not crow this day, before that thou shalt thrice deny that thou knowest me."

This prediction threw Peter into a frantic determination to prove his loyalty. Loyal as he knew himself to be, he was not humble enough to accept his Master's judgment that he might act disloyally. He thought his loyalty was due to his own efforts and that his determination and strength were sufficient to keep him faithful, come what might. He resolved to demonstrate this, with disastrous results.

In spite of the prediction, our Lord continued to put special confidence in Peter. He, with James and John, was taken into the inner recesses of the Garden of Gethsemane and set on watch. Peter, perhaps, seized this opportunity to speculate on how he could prove his loyalty, on how he would act under various circumstances. As his imagination wandered further and further afield, he drifted into a sleep filled with dreams of heroic exploits in defense of Him whom his slumbers left unprotected.

Twice our Lord awakened him with that searching question, "Simon, sleepest thou? couldest not thou watch one hour?" Both times, Peter, in spite of a determination to the contrary, slipped back into his romantic imaginings and dozed off again. Finally, he was aroused with the words, "Rise up, let us go; lo, he that betrayeth me is at hand." Before he could shake the sleep out of his eyes, Peter found himself in the midst of a bewildering scene. The eight disciples who had been left at the entrance of the Garden dashed up in full flight, closely pursued by the vanguard of the arrest party. The latter, confronted suddenly by Jesus' majestic calm, fell back and threw those behind them into confusion. At last, Judas stepped from the crowd and approached Jesus. "Hail, Master," and he kissed Him. This was the prearranged signal. The soldiers began to close in on our Lord.

Peter had watched all this without being able to compre-

hend its full significance or to decide what to do. Then the
question asked by one of the others, "Lord, shall we smite
with the sword?" precipitated Peter into impulsive action.
In a flash, his sword was drawn and he struck one of the
servants of the High Priest. Once again his Master cor-
rected him with quiet firmness, "Put up again thy sword
into his place," and He healed the wound the soldier had
received. Whereupon, Peter succumbed to his instinct
of self-preservation and fulfilled his promise to accompany Jesus to prison and death by taking to his heels.

In the shadows of the olive grove, as he heard the band
of soldiers move off, Peter pulled himself together. Already
he had repeatedly failed his Master in time of crisis. Still
he would not give up. Perchance there might yet be an
opportunity to help. So Peter followed afar off and, with
the aid of John, was able to enter the High Priest's courtyard. He sat down inconspicuously among the soldiers gathered around the fire.

Soon a serving-girl detected him. "This man was also
with him." The challenge intruded on Peter's brooding
over his recent failures and his speculations as to how he
could redeem himself. He brushed aside the threat to his
safety and to his freedom to help his Master. "Woman, I
know him not." It would never do to let himself be arrested. They were looking for witnesses against Jesus, and
they had no scruples against putting witnesses to torture.
Under the circumstances, a lie was justified. Thus reflecting, he stuck to his denial when challenged the second
time. The third accusation brought from him a vehement
repudiation, with oaths and curses, in a voice which rang

out across the courtyard to where the Prisoner was standing.

"And immediately, while he yet spake, the cock crew. And the Lord turned, and looked upon Peter. And Peter remembered the word of the Lord, how he had said unto him, Before the cock crow, thou shalt deny me thrice. And Peter went out, and wept bitterly."

Peter repented. He gave up his attempt to prove his loyalty by his own efforts. He did not rush up to Jesus with an immediate apology, an attempt to retract his denial, a demand for restoration into our Lord's favor. Nor did he seek to make up for his failure by openly avowing his discipleship, thus giving himself up to torture and death. He repented. He stopped thinking about himself, how he could win his Master's favor, how he could prove his loyalty. He thought how his denial had hurt Jesus. There stood Jesus in the hands of His enemies. All His friends had forsaken Him and fled except two. Now one of them had denied that he knew Him. Peter had done that to Jesus. Peter went out and wept bitterly.

They were not tears of self-pity. Peter was penitent, not just ashamed of himself. He was prepared to face himself as he was with honest self-appraisal. He went out into the night to be alone. He wanted to plumb the depths of his selfishness and sin. Why had he failed his Lord? What did this act of sin mean? What underlying selfishness did it indicate? Peter was penitent. He was not content with sorrow for the act of sin. He wanted to find and repudiate the selfishness which had caused him to act that way.

Peter avoided the mistake of viewing the act of sin as an accidental aberration, an impulsive slip of the tongue.

He might easily have so viewed it. He could even have gone on to justify it. He had been in a tight spot. Our Lord clearly did not want Peter arrested and killed. Already, He had indicated that He had more work for Peter to do, indicated it at the very time when He predicted Peter's denial. "When thou art converted, strengthen thy brethren." Yes, Peter could have built up a good case for himself, treating his denial as an unfortunate but unavoidable means of escaping from an intolerable situation.

Instead, Peter went back of the sin and asked why he was in a situation where the only escape was to deny Jesus. Was it not because he was trying to prove his loyalty? Presumption—that was Peter's sin. He took credit to himself for his loyalty. He felt that he could be faithful in his own strength. Jesus had prayed that Peter's faith fail not. Peter felt no necessity to pray about that. All he asked was an opportunity to demonstrate how faithful he was. Nor was this, Peter realized, a transient fit of bravado. He had walked into the situation which had led to His denial with his eyes open. One might even say he had walked in because his eyes were open. He had been warned specifically, but that warning had served only to stimulate his determination to prove himself loyal. He had repeatedly failed in the Garden of Gethsemane, but those failures had made him try the harder.

"I know him not." Those words by which Peter had first denied Jesus were closer to the truth than Peter had thought as he uttered them. Peter did not know Jesus fully, did not know how completely he had to depend on Him if he would remain faithful. Peter had always thought of their relationship as one of give and take. Jesus was the

Leader, Peter the follower; but he thought he had followed by his own power. At times, he felt a bit protective of Jesus, as he defended Him against an accusation by His enemies, as he extolled His virtues to a prospective convert. Peter knew that Jesus had much to give him. He was eager to learn all that the Master would teach him; he struggled hard to understand, to carry out, to anticipate His will. But Peter also thought that he had something to give Jesus; that he could do something for Him. That was why he had penetrated into the courtyard of the High Priest's house. He hoped for a chance to save Jesus. Instead, in order to save himself, he had cried, "I know him not."

This was the knowledge of himself that Peter gained, faced, accepted in the darkness of that night. Because he learned that lesson, he was now ready to put himself utterly in our Lord's hands. He was willing to be saved by Him. He was prepared to trust henceforth in Jesus, not in himself. Thereby, he became a surrendered soul through whom God could accomplish great things.

Had Peter's surrender come too late? The damage had been done. Jesus, as he soon learned, was to be put to death. How could Peter apologize to Him for the injury his denial had caused? Could Jesus forgive, and, even if so, could He assure Peter of His forgiveness? What would it matter anyway, once Jesus was dead? Perhaps, having faced his sin honestly, Peter was tempted to despair. If so, he rejected the temptation. His loyalty to our Lord was great enough to make him believe that somehow Jesus would find a way to forgive and to express His forgiveness. The penitent Peter was now humble enough to leave that, and everything else, in Jesus' hands. Peter knew Jesus loved him in spite of his faults. Peter accepted himself as he was and waited for God to act to make him better. He realized there was nothing he could do without God's help. But he also believed that help would be forthcoming.

Again, Judas gives us the contrast. He, also, sinned presumptuously that night and, by our Lord's question, "Judas, betrayest thou the Son of Man with a kiss?" was forced to face himself. Before he had given the treacherous kiss, he had convinced himself that he was doing his duty in handing over to the authorities a dangerous impostor, a deluded madman. The quiet dignity with which our Lord accepted His arrest convinced Judas that his Master was all that He claimed to be. Judas had betrayed the Messiah. Presumptuous pride had led him to condemn the Son of God and hand Him over to His enemies. Judas saw that he had sinned.

But Judas was too far gone in pride to repent. He would not accept the fact that he was a traitor. He would not believe that Jesus would forgive him, still less would he wait for that forgiveness. His first impulse was to undo the damage. Not Jesus' forgiveness but his own action must remove the sin. That alone could cure his hurt pride. The priests laughed at him when he brought back the money and demanded Jesus' release. "I have betrayed the innocent blood." "What is that to us? see thou to that." When he could not undo his crime, Judas yielded to despair. "He cast down the pieces of silver in the Temple and departed and went and hanged himself." Judas would not accept himself. Therefore, he could not accept the forgiving love of God. He would not repent.

Peter repented. He accepted himself just as he was with

all his presumption and sin. He did not try to hide the facts either from himself or from others. He was eager to admit them. Very significantly, we find him next with John, who had been present in the courtyard when Peter denied his Lord. John knew all about it. Peter felt more comfortable with John because of that. Probably he did not want to tell the others at that time about the way he had hurt Jesus. Their hearts were heavy enough already. But John knew. Peter felt he was not hiding anything from John, pretending to be better than he was. When with John, Peter experienced the relief that comes from a full and honest confession of sin. John could not yet in an official capacity assure Peter of God's forgiveness of his sin. John had not yet received that power from on high. He could, however, comfort Peter and encourage him to hope. And Peter was glad to share his burden of repented sin with John.

Nevertheless, Peter was too preoccupied with his thoughts of sin and penitence for him to believe when he saw the Empty Tomb. He wandered off alone to ponder this added grief of the disappearance of the Lord's body. Then, suddenly, before him stood the Master. We have no account of what occurred in that Appearance. We need none in order to know what happened. The Risen Christ came to tell Peter that his penitence was accepted, his sin forgiven. No one who has carried a burden of sin to God in confession and received through the lips of a priest God's gracious absolution finds it difficult to understand why Peter never told us the details of his first contact with the Risen Christ. The meeting of his penitence with God's forgiving love was too sacred, too intimate, to be revealed.

Although Peter never described his forgiveness, he must have spoken often of his sin. For the story of Peter's denial is in all the Gospels; and others would hardly have told it of him had he not led the way. Peter returned again and again to that sin in the courtyard which had revealed to him the extent of his presumption and had precipitated his utter surrender to Christ. It was his true conversion, out of which came the power to serve Christ faithfully for the remainder of his life. In that moment of soul-searching penitence, a saint was born. We can hear Peter tell the story and perhaps end it by saying, "That man, warming himself at the fire, denying his Master—that man is Peter. All the rest"—his apostleship, his ministry, his years of faithful service—"all the rest is the work of God."

VI

The Way of Prayer

And, behold, two of them went that same day to a village called Emmaus, which was from Jerusalem about threescore furlongs. And they talked together of all these things which had happened. And it came to pass, that, while they communed together and reasoned, Jesus himself drew near, and went with them. But their eyes were holden that they should not know him. And he said unto them, What manner of communications are these that ye have one to another, as ye walk, and are sad? And one of them, whose name was Cleopas, answering said unto him, Art thou only a stranger in Jerusalem, and hast not known the things which are come to pass there in these days? And he said unto them, What things? And they said unto him, Concerning Jesus of Nazareth, which was a prophet mighty in deed and word before God and all the people: and how the chief priests and our rulers delivered him to be condemned to death, and have crucified him. But we trusted that it had been he which should have redeemed Israel: and beside all this, today is the third day since these things were done. Yes, and certain women also of our company made us astonished, which were early at the sepulchre; and when they found not his body, they came, saying, that they had also seen a vision of angels, which said that he was alive. And certain of them which were with us went to the sepulchre, and found it even so as the women had said: but him they saw not. Then he said unto them, O fools, and slow of heart to believe all that the prophets have spoken: ought not Christ to have suffered these things, and to enter into his glory? And beginning at Moses and all the prophets, he expounded unto them in all the scriptures the things concerning himself. And they drew nigh unto the village, whither they went: and he made as though he would have gone further. But they constrained him, saying, Abide with us: for it is toward evening, and the day is far spent. And he went in to tarry with them. And it came to pass, as he sat at meat with them, he took bread, and blessed it, and brake, and gave to them. And their eyes were opened, and they knew him; and he vanished out of their sight. And they said one to another, Did not our heart burn within us, while he talked with us by the way, and while he opened to us the scriptures? And they rose up the same hour, and returned to Jerusalem. . . .

ST. LUKE 24:13-33.

Sometime during the course of the first Easter Day, two disciples left Jerusalem to go to Emmaus. One of them was Cleopas. The other is unnamed, and this person's identity has been the subject of much speculation throughout the centuries. Recently, it has been suggested[1] that the second disciple on the road to Emmaus was Mary, the wife of Cleopas, mentioned by St. John as one of the women on Calvary. (He calls her husband "Cleophas," but that is simply an alternate spelling of the same name.) This Mary has been traditionally identified with Mary the mother of James the Less and Joses mentioned in the synoptic accounts as being present on Calvary and as one of the holy women who visited the sepulchre early Easter morning.

This suggestion that Cleopas' companion was his wife Mary is, as far as we know, a pure guess with no weight of tradition behind it. It may, however, be an inspired

[1] Dorothy Sayers makes use of this suggestion in *The Man Born to Be King* and attributes it to the Bishop of Ripon.

guess. There is some evidence in its favor. The fact that the companion is unnamed points to a woman rather more than to a man. The primary purpose of the accounts of the Resurrection in the minds of the Evangelists was to give the testimony to the fact that it occurred. Since in Judaism women could not be official witnesses, it was not particularly important that their names be given. This may be the reason why St. Paul, in listing those to whom Christ appeared, omits the name of Mary Magdalene. Once we question the unreasoned assumption that the unnamed disciple must be a man, we can see that there is much to be said for the hypothesis that she was Cleopas' wife. It brings the episode to life at several points. Without, therefore, claiming historical certainty for it, we shall use it for what it is worth in making the story vivid.

To begin with, it supplies a much needed motive for the departure of two disciples from Jerusalem on Easter Day. We know that they were aware of the Empty Tomb and the message of the angel. One would think that only a very impelling motive could overcome the natural curiosity that would tend to keep them in Jerusalem awaiting developments.

Assume that these two disciples were Cleopas and his wife and at once the motive is clear. Let us reconstruct the events of Easter morning. The first to bring the news of the Empty Tomb to Jerusalem were not the holy women, but the guard which had been on watch. These were not Roman soldiers. Pilate refused to take responsibility for guarding Jesus' grave, saying to the chief priests, "Ye have a watch: go your way, make it as sure as ye can." He expected them to use the Temple soldiery, which they did. How little concept these men had of military discipline and honor is shown by their willingness to be bribed into accusing themselves of having slept on guard, an offense which, in the Roman army, would have been punished by death.

One can readily imagine what these "soldiers" did when confronted with the Empty Tomb. A graveyard is at best a scary place in the early hours of the morning. They were watching the sepulchre of a notorious Person whose popularity, miracles, and claim to be the Messiah had caused the authorities to handle Him with a caution which amounted almost to awe. They had even feared that He might be dangerous after His death. Suddenly, this fear came true. To the accompaniment of an earthquake and the appearance of an angel, the stone was rolled back from the sepulchre and its emptiness revealed. Of course, the guard rushed for Jerusalem in panic flight, shouting at the top of their lungs to every passer-by that the tomb was empty, that the body of Jesus had disappeared.

This would seem to be the only possible explanation of the action of the authorities when they learned the news. Why did they not quash the whole business by sending the guard back with instructions to replace the stone and the seals and to maintain that the grave had never been disturbed? That would have been the simplest and most effective denial of the untoward event. But this course was not open to them because the indiscretion of the guard had already made the Empty Tomb a matter of common knowledge. It was too late to deny the fact. Some other explanation had to be found, and the guards' fear of punishment for their publication of the news may have been a more potent inducement than the bribe in persuading them to circulate the false report that His disciples came by night and stole Him away while they slept. This was a very feeble explanation and centuries later St. Augustine was to have much fun at its expense, pointing out how it rests on the testimony of sleeping witnesses. Under the circumstances, however, it seemed the best that could be devised, and the soldiers were sent out to spread it.

The fact that the emptiness of the sepulchre was too well known in Jerusalem for the authorities to be able to deny it outright is, as Frank Morison shows,[2] the reason why there is no reference to the women's visit to the Empty Tomb in the sermons recorded for us in the Acts. There was no need to assert and prove the fact that the tomb was empty, for that had been common knowledge for weeks. The admission that some of their party had visited the sepulchre, on the other hand, would have weakened the Apostles' case. It would have given color to their opponents' contention that the disciples had robbed the tomb. Hence, they kept secret for the time being the women's corroboration of what everyone admitted anyway.

Now let us return to what was happening among our Lord's followers on Easter morning. The women, except Mary Magdalene, returned with the news of the Empty Tomb and the angel's message. Mary the wife of Cleopas, be it remembered, was one of the women. The disciples gathered to discuss the unexpected turn of events. While thus engaged, the report which the soldiers were spreading in the city reached their ears. What would be its effect

[2] In *Who Moved the Stone?*

on Cleopas? Our Lord's disciples were being charged with having robbed the sepulchre. His wife had been at the tomb that morning. If that fact was known by the authorities, she was in imminent danger of being charged with the removal of Jesus' body.

In the light of this analysis, Cleopas ceases to be a mere name and becomes a definite personality whose actions can be understood. He was a cautious man who, when confronted with danger, blustered into precipitous action. To get his wife away from Jerusalem was his immediate determination and, overriding her mild protests with a torrent of reiteration that this was the only course, he bustled her off. Once clear of the city, he began to expatiate at great length on the foolishness of having ever become associated with the Galilean and His lost cause. Mary's gentle reminders of the wonder of His teaching and the hope He had given them served only to exasperate Cleopas the more, as did her persistent clinging to the "idle tale" that she had seen an angel who said that Jesus was alive.[8] One suspects that when St. Luke tells us that "they talked together of all these things which had happened" and "communed together and reasoned," he is euphemistically describing what was, on the part of Cleopas at least, a heated discussion.

[8] In St. Matthew, we are told that the holy women saw our Lord as they returned to Jerusalem. This is the one Appearance referred to in the New Testament which is not included in this book. The brief passage in St. Matthew, with its phrase, they "held him by the feet," looks as if it were a generalization of the Appearance to Mary Magdalene. That is how we have treated it. An additional Appearance to the other holy women does not fit into the scheme of the story at all well, and it would seem to be contradicted by St. Luke 24:24, "But him they saw not." The "they" refers strictly to Peter and John, but Cleopas has just grudgingly admitted that they found things "even so as the women had said." This makes it clear that Cleopas had not heard of anyone's having seen the Risen Christ, though he had heard the women's report.

This may well be the rather surprising background of the third Resurrection Appearance. As we said at the start, it is only a guess, but it does fit the few facts we have and seems to give them a plausible explanation. Nor is it in the least inconsistent with our Lord's having revealed Himself to them. Neither Cleopas' fear and flight nor his wife's acquiescence in them was a genuine rejection of Christ. They were bewildered and confused. Deep in their hearts, they wanted above all to do God's will, but they had no clear idea what God wanted of them.

They may be taken as beginners in the Christian life, representing the two chief temperamental types; Cleopas the aggressive, domineering, practical, and Mary the gentle, hesitant, imaginative. Both types now find themselves in the same situation and are rescued by the same means. They had recently been converted to Christ and espoused His cause with enthusiasm. Then His crucifixion and death blighted their conversion hopes. All was not going to be happy ever after, as new converts always seem to expect. The initial fervors were over and they were brought up against the hard realities of the spiritual life. The significance of the Empty Tomb was so far above their heads that there was no chance of their comprehending it. Its discovery simply added to their confusion and danger. They were offended and afraid. Their first impulse was to give up and they dashed off in headlong flight.

Our Lord pursued them. He picked them up where they were and went along with them, slowly opening their minds to the truth, until at last He could reveal Himself to them. Viewed in this way, the Appearance on the road to Emmaus has an important meaning for us. It assures us that, though we be novices in the spiritual life, though we be confused and bewildered, though, as a result, we actually start off on the wrong track, we can still be found by Christ, if—and this is the whole point—if we are faithful to the ordinary ways of prayer.

For the manner of our Lord's Appearance is in every detail a perfect example of an acted-out discursive meditation. Such meditation should be, for most beginners, the staple of their private prayer life. St. Teresa said that no soul could be lost who gave fifteen minutes a day to meditation. Mental prayer is hard work, of course; most worthwhile things are. But if it is practiced regularly it does, from time to time, produce genuine insights into God's love and His will. These will not for us take the form of seeing the Risen Christ; nor of ecstatic experiences. Nonetheless, they will be real contacts with our Lord, and in coming to us He will follow the same pattern on our far lower level that we find in His Appearance on the road to Emmaus.

Note, first, that Jesus drew near the disciples and went with them. This is the primary point that we must realize about our meditations. As we begin them, it is not we who draw near to Christ. He comes to us. He is always coming, always at hand. When we compose ourselves for prayer, we simply turn and pay attention to Him. We may not recognize Him at first. But we can know by faith and experience that He is with us. We go along with Him.

Jesus opened the conversation by asking what was on their minds. He began with the difficulties which were uppermost in their thoughts. He wants us to bring our problems to Him. Nor is He in the least offended when we present them in our own words and in the way that we see them. We can hear the scorn in Cleopas' voice and see the withering glance he gave his wife, when he said, "Yea, and certain women also of our company made us astonished, which were early at the sepulchre; and when they found not his body, they came, saying, that they had also seen a vision of angels, which said that he was alive." Our Lord does not want us to assume a pious or formal pose as we speak to Him. He wants us simply and naturally to open our hearts.

He, in turn, opened to them the Scriptures. He expounded to them the things concerning Himself. This is the part that the Bible passage should play in our meditation. Having composed ourselves and realized Christ's presence, we turn to the subject-matter on which we are to make our discursive meditation. This will usually be a few verses from the Bible. At first it is well to use the Gospels, since they are the most fruitful source of meditation material. If we are wise, we choose the subject the night before and read the Bible passage over slowly and carefully before going to bed. This plants it in the subconscious where it can take root during sleep and be the more vivid when used in the time of prayer.

The purpose of the discursive part of the meditation is to draw out of the Bible passage a message for oneself. If it describes a scene in our Lord's life, we do well to put ourselves into it, identifying ourselves with one or another of the characters and letting Christ speak to us as He did to them. Or we can identify ourselves with our Lord and ask how, in terms of our own lives, we can imitate the character He displays. If the verses on which we are thinking are from His teaching, we can treat them as a personal message to us, and consider how we can carry out the advice He gives. The snares to avoid are speculation on the subject-matter in general, impersonal terms, and sentimental musing on an event that happened long ago. Meditation is not an exercise in biblical exegesis or a pious reverie. It is letting Christ speak to us through the words of the Gospel. We may not always get a clear and inspiring message, and when we do, we may not find it emotionally stimulating. Yet, if we are consistently trying to let Christ open to us the Scriptures, we shall find our hearts burning within us more often than we have any right to expect.

We now reach the crucial moment of the meditation. Failure to do the right thing at this point is fatal. Most people who say they cannot meditate, or who consider it useless, have consistently made a mistake here. They have treated the discursive reasoning on the Bible passage as the meditation, whereas, in fact, it is only the preliminary. Speculation, even when it is brought down to the point of personal application, is not prayer. We pray not with our minds but with our wills. Prayer is not thinking of God but responding to Him. As soon as we have distilled from our subject-matter the message God is giving to us, we must answer Him, speaking to Him in the second person as friend to friend, assuring Him of our purpose to do His will.

The disciples reached this moment of crisis when they arrived at Emmaus. Their journey thither was the discursive part of the meditation. During it they learned much and gained a new insight into the meaning of recent events. They began to understand that Christ ought "to have suffered these things, and to enter into his glory." But they did not recognize Christ. There was no personal contact with Him. Had they stopped at that, the instruction would have produced no commensurate results in their lives. If, when they reached their house, they had thanked the Stranger for His talk and bidden Him farewell, they would never have learned who He was. They would have missed their vocation to be witnesses of the Resurrection.

As it was, "They constrained him, saying, Abide with us: for it is toward evening and the day is far spent. And he went in to tarry with them." They took Him right into their home. Mary rushed off to the kitchen to prepare food and set it on the table before Him. Cleopas engaged in friendly person-to-person conversation as host to the Risen Christ. So must we invite Him into our hearts, put what we have to offer at His service, engage in intimate colloquy with Him. This is what turns the discourse into prayer, the insight into action. We respond to Jesus in terms of the message He has given us, making appropriate prayers of faith, love, hope, penitence, thanksgiving, and adoration. We see how we can express these attitudes more adequately in our daily living and in our relationship with our fellow-men. Perhaps we may even be able to make some small resolution as a token offering of our intent to serve Christ in this way.

But we are not the garrulous host who does all the talking. We listen to our holy Guest, we watch Him, we sit quietly in His presence. From time to time, He will make Himself known to us—not in His Risen Body made visible as at Emmaus—but in a more spiritual, though no less certain, way. It will be through some simple gesture like the

breaking of bread. A word, a phrase will suddenly come to
life with new meaning, a power will well up in us from a
hidden source, a restful peace will engulf the soul. Human
language can never quite describe the experience:

> The love of Jesus, what it is
> None but His loved ones know.

These contacts are both rare and fleeting. We must not
demand them; we hardly dare expect them. God knows
best when to bestow them and when to ask us to meditate
faithfully for weeks, for months, perhaps for years, without tasting this touch of Reality. Then, suddenly, when
we least anticipate it, it comes. Our eyes are open and we
know Him; and He vanishes out of our sight. He is gone
as soon as He is recognized. For it is His touch, not our
cogitation, that produces the experience. Indeed, He can
come only when all our mental and emotional processes are
still, are inactive, are held in deliberate abeyance by an act
of our wills holding fast to Him. As soon as our minds,
reflecting on the experience, start to recognize Him and
our hearts leap up with joy, He is gone. We must not con-
fuse the afterglow with the touch itself. Ideas that occur
to us at those times are not to be considered direct in-
spirations from God. They come, at least in part, out of our
own heads and must be verified by independent evidence to
show that they are God's will before they are acted upon.
The sweetness that follows the contact must not be clung
to nor sought for its own sake. Christ comes, yes. But He
vanishes as soon as He is known.

Nevertheless, out of our meditations do come a new
orientation. The disciples arose and returned to Jerusalem.

There they found Christ again in the experience of the Christian fellowship. As they hurried along the road, they reminded each other of the chief points of the discourse which they had had with Christ, fixing them in their minds. So we, after our meditations, turn to our daily tasks with a renewed determination to serve Christ in them, and take along with us a thought or two which we have found helpful, to remind us of the contact we have had with Him.

Meditation is not the highest form of prayer. It is higher than vocal prayer, the mere recitation of set forms of devotion. But it is the lowest form of mental prayer. For most beginners, however, it is the first step, a necessary discipline that leads on to the higher forms. If we meditate properly, remembering that the direct colloquy with Christ is the main element, and, consequently, getting through the preliminaries as fast as we can, and abiding in the colloquy as long as possible, the Holy Spirit will be able to guide us through meditation itself to the next steps, when we are ready for them. For above meditation is affective prayer. The difference between them is that in the latter the discursive part of the meditation is shortened to the point of vanishing. A simple idea, of God's love or mercy or majesty, starts us at once responding with acts of will. The still higher form of prayer, acquired recollection, is but the logical outcome of affective prayer. In it, our acts of will are no longer varied but become fused in a single glance of loving regard by which we cling to God.

These forms of prayer are called "acquired" because, with the help of grace, they can be consciously cultivated. We can direct the attention of our minds to God and to some aspect of His revelation of Himself. Occasionally, as we have seen, the colloquy and acts of affective prayer will arise spontaneously from this consideration. Often, however, they will not. At such times we should make them deliberately with our wills, in spite of the deadness of our feelings and in the teeth of the distractions of our minds. We should memorize simple exclamations of faith, hope, love, and penitence, so that they will be available for use when our hearts suggest no spontaneous affections. This making of "forced" acts of prayer is essential to progress through periods of doubt and spiritual dryness. Such prayers are not insincere because we do not feel them, since prayer is the work, not of the emotions, but of the will. By willing to believe in God, to trust Him, to love Him, when we do not feel like it, we permit the Holy Spirit to lead us to the highest level of the spiritual life to which we can attain by a conscious co-operation with grace.

Beyond lies infused contemplation. That is a pure gift of God. We cannot win it for ourselves, either by our efforts or by our merits. In this life, it is reserved for those for whom it has been prepared. But never doubt, they are to be found only among those who have been faithful in the lower forms of prayer, allowing the Holy Spirit to bring the virtues of faith, hope, and love to full fruition in their souls and to make operative His gifts of wisdom and understanding. Infused contemplation is the experience in which God Himself takes the soul into His arms and presses it to His Heart. Perhaps we shall never receive this favor while still on earth. It is, however, the eternal joy of all the redeemed in heaven. Hence, it is the true end of the way of prayer. It is the goal toward which we set out when we begin regularly to practice the humble art of meditation.

VII

The Church at Worship

And as they thus spake, Jesus himself stood in the midst of them, and saith unto them, Peace be unto you. But they were terrified and affrighted, and supposed that they had seen a spirit. And he said unto them, Why are ye troubled? and why do thoughts arise in your hearts? Behold my hands and my feet, that it is I myself: handle me, and see; for a spirit hath not flesh and bones, as ye see me have. And when he had thus spoken, he shewed them his hands and his feet. And while they yet believed not for joy, and wondered, he said unto them, Have ye here any meat? And they gave him a piece of a broiled fish, and of an honeycomb. And he took it, and did eat it before them. And he said unto them, These are the words which I spake unto you, while I was yet with you, that all things must be fulfilled, which were written in the law of Moses, and in the prophets, and in the psalms, concerning me. Then opened he their understanding, that they might understand the scriptures, and said unto them, Thus it is written, and thus it behoved Christ to suffer, and to rise from the dead the third day: And that repentance and remission of sins should be preached in his name among all nations, beginning at Jerusalem. And ye are witnesses of these things.

ST. LUKE 24:36-48.

Then the same day at evening, being the first day of the week, when the doors were shut where the disciples were assembled for fear of the Jews, came Jesus and stood in the midst, and saith unto them, Peace be unto you. And when he had so said, he shewed unto them his hands and his side. Then were the disciples glad, when they saw the Lord.

ST. JOHN 20:19-20.

83

When the two disciples returned from Emmaus, they found the door of the Upper Room locked. The same fear which had precipitated their flight caused the assembled disciples to guard themselves against intruders. Perhaps they were unduly alarmed. The authorities probably were content to leave them unmolested as long as they remained in hiding and refrained from contradicting the official report that they had stolen our Lord's body from the tomb. Silence on their part made it easier for the false report to be accepted and believed; whereas their arrest and trial would have produced a vehement denial, which might have weakened the case against them. The authorities were content to win the argument by default. This accomplished most satisfactorily their real objective, the hushing up of the whole affair. They wanted Jesus to be forgotten as quickly as possible. Hence they had no intention of reopening and prolonging the excitement by ferreting out the disciples.

Nevertheless, the disciples' fear, though it may have been unfounded, was real. They believed themselves in imminent danger of arrest. In the teeth of this fear, they assembled in the Upper Room. They felt they had to meet. This shows how definitely the Master had planted the idea of fellowship in their minds. Response to the call to follow Him had made them participants in a common life. The first corollary of their love of Him was that they love one another. Much of their new Christian character had been molded by their mutual association. Growth in intimacy with our Lord was achieved by closer integration into the group, not by particular friendship with Him. It was Judas, the individualist, who would not surrender to the fellowship, who became the traitor.

The disciples knew they needed each other, not only for mutual support and assurance, but because they had learned to expect to find the Master in and with each other. They cautiously threaded their way to the place of meeting. Thither Cleopas and his companion returned after our Lord had called them back. They knocked at the door and were identified. Bursting into the room, they cried, "We have seen the Lord."

They were greeted with the words, "The Lord is risen indeed, and hath appeared to Simon." It is interesting to note in passing that someone other than Peter made this statement. Hitherto, Peter had always been the most outspoken of the Apostles, asserting and reiterating his opinion, loudly proclaiming his faithfulness. His penitence had changed all that. He had already told the group of our Lord's Appearance to him. Now he was content silently to confirm the testimony with a nod and to leave to others the defense and discussion of it.

Discussion there doubtless was. Many must have found the truth hard to believe. Cleopas and his companion elaborated their confirming testimony. Some were convinced. Others plied them with questions. Others expressed doubt and incredulity.

Is not this a convincing picture, on a higher plane but still clearly recognizable, of normal Church life? There, on Easter night, were gathered all the types which one finds in the average congregation on any Sunday. Some—Peter, Mary Magdalene, Cleopas and his companion—have already had a vivid experience of the Risen Lord. There are usually a few in any Christian gathering whose faith rests on a deep experience of its truth which has been vouchsafed to them. They can bear witness with assurance. They have seen the Lord.

Others, like John and our Lord's Mother, are men and women of great faith. Without having seen, they have believed. Their full-hearted response has given them an insight into the truth. They understand, because they know God. They need neither a vivid personal experience nor the testimony of others to convince them. They are the mystics who find the truth by the hidden path of love.

Others, still, believe on the basis of the testimony of those who have seen. They consider the witnesses trustworthy and accept the truth on their authority. These today are the ones who have responded faithfully to the normal process of Christian nurture. They have been brought up in the Faith, or converted to it by evangelization and instruction. They may not have had any exceptional experience of the validity of their belief; probably they cannot give a reasoned defense of it. It is enough for them to know that our Lord's accredited and authorized witnesses so testify. They constitute the majority of faithful in any congregation.

Finally, there are those who find it hard to believe. Doubts and questions assail their minds. They are not hostile, nor are they indifferent. They want to learn. They long to believe. But they cannot convince themselves of the truth. These are the earnest seekers after God, who do not yet realize that they have arrived. Their efforts to find Him hide from them the stupendous truth that they have already been found by Him.

Outside is the hostile world, exerting its ponderous influence to keep them away from the fellowship. On the first Easter this influence took the form of fear of persecution. So it was to continue for the first three centuries, and off and on, here and there, ever since. Perhaps in our day, right in our country, we shall see it happen again. The veneer of tolerance of Christianity is far thinner than we realize. The threat to it which caused the Second World War has temporarily been averted. But only a foolish optimist would hold that thereby the nation has been converted to Christ. The forces of persecution may arise at any moment, and the next time they may come from within our borders. For the present, however, the world's hostility takes the form of scornful indifference. This is an even more potent deterrent than persecution. It takes determination to rise above the dead level of enervating sloth. Yet our faithfulness is not stimulated by the thrill that comes from braving the danger of martyrdom. It does not seem particularly heroic to be laughed at.

In spite of their fear, in spite of their varying degrees of faith, the disciples gathered in the Upper Room on the first Easter night. And·those who gathered saw the Lord. For suddenly the discussion terminated in a breathless hush. Jesus stood in the midst and said, "Peace be unto you."

This may be called our Lord's first official Appearance. Three times before, the Risen Christ had shown Himself to one or another of His disciples. These, however were private Appearances. Each had a specific purpose, meeting the particular need of the person concerned. Mary Magdalene was lifted from the bewildered frustration of the faithful following of her vocation to the level of intimacy with the Risen Lord. Peter was relieved of the burden of repented sin that he might be restored to his place in the Apostolic circle. Cleopas and his companion were rescued from their misguided flight and brought back to the fellowship. In each instance, the private Appearance was a necessary step in preparing the recipient to participate in the experience of the Upper Room.

The Appearance there had no purpose except to manifest the reality of our Lord's Resurrection. Only a public Appearance could do that. Historical truth is established by the concurring testimony of many witnesses. The fact of the Resurrection measures up to that criterion. It does not rest solely on the claim of certain individuals that somewhere, off by themselves, they had an esoteric contact with the Risen Christ. Such a claim might have been open to the charge that it was the product of self-hypnosis or self-deception. It would be too insecure a foundation on which to rest the Gospel of man's redemption. Our Lord does not ask us to believe on the basis of any individual's revelation. The authority to which He appeals and through which He manifests Himself is the corporate witness of the faithful.

They all saw Him. They all heard Him. As each glanced hastily about the room, he saw that all the others were participating in exactly the same experience. All were shrinking back from the terrible majesty of that Figure, flattening themselves against the wall. Love and joy struggled with fear and incredulity. They were overwhelmed by the impossible wonder of it.

"Why are ye troubled? and why do thoughts arise in your hearts? Behold my hands and my feet, that it is I myself:

handle me and see; for a spirit hath not flesh and bones, as ye see me have." He stretched out His arms toward them. They crept forward. One touched Him, then another, and another. It was true. The arms were solid; the flesh firm. He was not a spirit, a ghost. He was a real Man in a real body.

Still they believed not, for joy. God allowed every last vestige of doubt to attack their minds in order that it might be refuted. "Have ye here any meat?" One of the women gathered up the fragments of a meal, some broiled fish and a bit of honeycomb. With what homely material things was the most gigantic spiritual truth established! They watched Him take the food up in His fingers. He put it into His mouth. He chewed and swallowed it.

His Risen Body was a real body, no longer in need of nourishment, but capable of performing the natural function of eating when He willed to do so, manifestable to the ordinary human senses of sight, hearing, and touch, when He wished it to be. Our Lord carefully demonstrated all this to His assembled disciples. He proved it up to the hilt. He drove the fact home. He had not passed through the portal of death to become a disembodied spirit. He had risen in the flesh.

"It is I myself." These words show the significance that our Lord's physical Resurrection had in His mind and those of His disciples. It was the proof of His personal survival. Man as we know him is a combination of body and soul. Without either component, he would cease to be man. He would become something different, either a corpse or a ghost. Survival in either or both of these forms was of no interest to the practical-minded Jew. For under those circumstances he realized that it would not be he who survived. In the Old Testament, before the hope of the Resurrection was born in Judaism, the Jews expected to go on existing in Sheol, but that was a gloomy place where disembodied souls flitted aimlessly about in the darkness. Only when faith in the Resurrection of the body took root in Jewish thought did the life after death become something which could be anticipated with joy.

As usual, the pendulum swung too far and there were those among our Lord's contemporaries who thought of the risen life as a continual round of banquets and carnal delights. This is the concept of the Resurrection which the Sadducees sought to ridicule when they asked our Lord whose wife the much married woman would be when she and her seven husbands rose from the dead. The Master disposed of this aspect of the question decisively. "In the Resurrection they neither marry, nor are given in marriage, but are as the angels of God in heaven." The joys of the future life are not to be an intensification of the fleshly pleasures of this. Many of our natural functions in this life are necessitated by the limitations of our earthly existence. These will be transcended in the life to come.

In the Resurrection, our bodies will be changed. They will become the perfect expression of our souls. Our risen bodies will not need to be nourished, rested, or laboriously moved from place to place. But they will be real bodies, carrying with them the personal characteristics, though not the limitations, of our present bodies. Because we shall have these bodies, we shall be men. For all eternity, we shall be what we were created to be, a soul and body fused in a single unity. We shall not survive in halves. We shall be ourselves.

The Christian, accordingly, does not consider the body to be a prison-house of the soul, something to be escaped from, so that the spirit may soar to heavenly heights. Our present sin-corrupted body is; but that is because it is disordered by sin, not because it is a body. Far from being essentially evil, our bodies are eternally an integral part of us. Asceticism and mortification aim at putting off the old man with his affections and lusts; that is, the disordered aspects of our present nature, in order that we may put on the "new man." Throughout the process, the aim and ideal is to be men, creatures which are a combination of body and soul.

Christ the Firstfruits of the Resurrection confirms this hope. He rose from the dead in a human body. It had qualities not found in earthly bodies. It could pass through locked doors; it could appear and disappear at will. It was beyond the reach of suffering and death. Yet it was continuous with the body which had been laid in the grave. Its features and voice were recognized by His friends; and they saw in its hands and feet the mark of the nails.

With this Appearance the Resurrection becomes a well-authenticated historical fact. Our Lord demonstrated the reality of His Risen Body before many witnesses. Forty days later, they told the world of their experience, giving the graphic details which have come down to us. All of them were present in Jerusalem at the time, and all must have been in agreement as to what took place. What would not the authorities have given if they could have found just one person who had been present in the Upper Room who denied that the episode occurred, or contradicted some essential part of it? How they would have capitalized on that one dissenting testimony to cast doubt and discredit on the story of the others! Yet there is not the faintest rumor of such an argument's being used against the Christians. Clearly, the verdict of the eye-witnesses must have been unanimous. Very few historical facts are so firmly established.

Once they were convinced by the evidence of their senses, confirmed by their mutual perception of the same series of events, "then were the disciples glad, when they saw the Lord." St. Matthew, in his account of another public Appearance, says, "When they saw him, they worshipped him." That was the inevitable response to His Presence. Drawn together in a self-forgetting fellowship, they lifted up their hearts in joy and thanksgiving to God. Here we have the two essential elements of corporate worship—the Presence of God objectively manifested, and a congregation united in adoration of Him.

Worship demands the objective Presence of God. God is, of course, present everywhere. But for the purpose of worship being present everywhere is about the same as being present nowhere. In order to be worshiped, God must be present here. He must, in a special sense, be in this place. To worship God does not mean that we are to adore Him in some vague and ethereal manner. For we have bodies, and we must use our bodies in worship as in any other human activity. Our bodies require a center on which to focus, toward which to direct their acts of reverence. God has given us what we need, a definite manifestation of

Himself on the material level, at a specific point in place
and time.

Under the Old Covenant, the center was the Temple at
Jerusalem, and, within the Temple, the holy of holies. This
was not a human invention. The Jews did not say to themselves, we must have a center of worship; therefore, let us
choose a site and build a temple there. God permitted David
to acquire the site of the Temple and He indicated it by
staying the pestilence, in answer to David's prayer, at the
threshing place of Araunah the Jebusite. God inspired
Solomon to build there the Temple and to place within the
veil of the holy of holies the Ark of the Covenant, the
mercy-seat. God placed His Name there. He made it the
center of the manifestations of His glory. "The Lord is in
his holy Temple; let all the earth keep silence before Him."

In establishing the New Covenant, our Lord took bread
and having given thanks, He brake it and said, "This is my
Body." Likewise, He gave thanks over the wine, saying,
"This is my Blood." "This do in remembrance of me." Thus
He provided the new holy of holies. Now no longer is it
hidden, for by His death "the veil of the Temple was rent
in twain from the top to the bottom." Now no longer
is it to be found only in Jerusalem. God's Presence is lo-
calized just as objectively and definitely in terms of elements of our material world, but the place may be any altar
before which a congregation gathers and where a duly authorized priest repeats in our Lord's name the words and
actions of the Last Supper.

Like the disciples in the Upper Room, we may gather
Sunday by Sunday to be with the Risen Christ and to lose
ourselves in an act of worship. To participate fully, how-

ever, we must constantly remember that worship is a corporate act. In that, it differs from private devotion. In worship, we are not individually and severally offering our personal love and praise to God. Still less are we seeking some benefit for ourselves, either a material favor, or a spiritual inspiration. Such things may often result from worship, but they can never be its conscious object and motivation.

In worship, we are the Church, the Body through which Christ makes Himself present at that particular time and place, in which He offers to the Father once more the perfect act of love which He consummated on Calvary. He can thus manifest Himself because we are there and because we supply Him with the raw materials, the bread and wine. It is His act, but since we are the means through which He acts, we are taken up and we participate in it. It becomes our act, not because we perform it, but because He performs it through us, and not through us as an aggregate of separate individuals, but through us as a congregation engaged in a single corporate act, an act of His Body the Church. Until we recapture that sense of being caught up in a common activity which is not our own, but Christ's, acting through us as a congregation, which is aimed not at edifying us but at offering praise to God, we shall never discover the secret or the joy of worship.

Against the background of that worship Christ opened the disciples' "understanding, that they might understand the scriptures." It is only in such an environment that the Scriptures can be understood. For the Bible, both the Old Testament, which is what our Lord meant by the Scriptures, and even more, the New Testament, is an account of the activity of God. It recounts much of human history; it records the whole gamut of human response from the basest sins to the highest aspirations. Yet these are secondary. The protagonist of the mighty saga is God, God redeeming the world. Only those who know by experience that God is at work on earth, that He chooses, calls, and incorporates men into Himself—and the highest and clearest form of that experience is worship—only those are in a position to understand the Scriptures.

Nor do they understand them as individuals. Each of us is capable of grasping but a fragment of the divine truth. Only God can know God. Only the perfect human mind of God Incarnate can know all that God has revealed to men. Only the mind of Christ can fully understand the Scriptures. "Neither knoweth any man the Father, save the Son, and he to whomsoever the Son will reveal him." How does the Son reveal Him? Christ continues to speak through His Body the Church. This means the whole Church; not any individual in the Church, not any group within the Church, but the consensus of all the faithful everywhere at all times. It is to the Church united to her divine Head, as were the disciples gathered in the Upper Room about the Risen Christ, that He has committed the understanding of the Scriptures.

We have already noted that to the disciples on the road to Emmaus Christ "expounded . . . in all the scriptures the things concerning himself." We have correlated that to the insight which comes from time to time in private prayer. That also is a truth of the spiritual life, but a very different truth from the one we are now considering. To Cleopas and his companion, Christ expounded the Scriptures before He revealed Himself, in order to get them into the condition which would permit Him to reveal Himself. The objective was not to give them an authoritative understanding of the Scriptures, but to draw them to Himself. This is always the purpose of private prayer and private revelation. It meets the individual's needs. But it results, when properly received and interpreted, not in sending the individual off to teach in his own name, to found his own Church. Rather, it sends him back into the fellowship, as the disciples "rose up the same hour, and returned to Jerusalem, and found the eleven gathered together, and them that were with them." Having by private prayer been led back to the Church, they then participated in its understanding of the Scriptures.

To the assembled Church Christ said, "Ye are witnesses of these things." To the disciples as a group, He committed the official testimony. That is the keynote of this Appearance. Just as it was in the presence of the Church that Christ demonstrated with great care the reality of His Resurrection, so to the Church He gave the responsibility and the power to witness to the Gospel from generation to generation. Our Faith rests not on the testimony of an individual, or even of a group of individuals. It rests on the witness of the Church, intimately united to Christ in living worship. We know that what it teaches is true. For the Mind of the Church is the Mind of Christ.

VIII

Spiritual Combat

But Thomas, one of the twelve, called Didymus, was not with them when Jesus came. The other disciples therefore said unto him, We have seen the Lord. But he said unto them, Except I shall see in his hands the print of the nails, and put my finger into the print of the nails, and thrust my hand into his side, I will not believe. And after eight days again his disciples were within, and Thomas with them: then came Jesus, the doors being shut, and stood in the midst, and said, Peace be unto you. Then saith he to Thomas, Reach hither thy finger, and behold my hands; and reach hither thy hand and thrust it into my side: and be not faithless, but believing. And Thomas answered and said unto him, my Lord and my God. Jesus saith unto him, Thomas, because thou hast seen me, thou hast believed: blessed are they that have not seen, and yet have believed. And many other signs truly did Jesus in the presence of his disciples, which are not written in this book: but these are written, that ye might believe that Jesus is the Christ, the Son of God; and that believing ye might have life through his name.

ST. JOHN 20:24-31.

Thomas "was not with them when Jesus came." He was absent from the Upper Room on the first Easter night. He did not share in the Church's experience of the Risen Lord. Neither could he bring himself to believe on the strength of the Apostles' testimony. As a result, he remained doubtful of the Resurrection. "Except I shall see in his hands the print of the nails, and put my finger into the print of the nails, and thrust my hand into his side, I will not believe." Blinded by his doubt, he was plunged for a while into spiritual darkness.

We do not know why Thomas was absent from the Upper Room. Two possibilities are open. It may have been his own fault. Or he may have been hindered by circumstances beyond his control. Since we have no way of choosing between these alternatives, and since each represents a situation in which we frequently find ourselves, let us explore them both and see what they can teach us.

He may simply have stayed away. We can easily think of excuses by which he could have justified his action to himself. Perhaps he was ashamed of himself. When our Lord had announced that He was going into Judea to raise Lazarus, His disciples had sought to deter Him. "Master, the Jews of late sought to stone thee; and goest thou thither again?" Nevertheless, our Lord had asserted that He would go. Then Thomas had said, "Let us also go, that we may die with him." Brave words. But when the soldiers arrested Jesus in the Garden, Thomas fled with the rest of the disciples. If Thomas was a sensitive soul, somewhat unduly concerned about his reputation, he may have been reluctant to face the others. He may have feared that they would taunt him with the contrast between his heroic boast and his subsequent conduct. Of course, they would have done nothing of the sort. Not only would charity have restrained them, but each of the disciples was too keenly aware of his own failings to fault Thomas for his. Nevertheless, Thomas may not have trusted them and may have hesitated to risk their scorn. He may have preferred to keep by himself.

Again, his grief at the Master's death may have plunged him into an apathetic despondency. What was the use of carrying on? The cause had failed. The Leader was dead. Why go through the motions? No one had commanded Thomas to go to the Upper Room. He did not feel like going. Nothing would be accomplished if he went. He would stay at home.

Or he may have yielded to that most subtle of all temptations, the desire to be alone with God. Herein the devil disguises himself as an angel of light. There are times when the soul must retire into solitude that God may speak to the heart. But the spiritual life is not simply a flight of the alone to the Alone. God comes via the community as well, and there are times when the soul must take its place in the fellowship if it is to know God. Both private and public prayer are essential to healthy spiritual growth. If either may be said to be the more fundamental, it is participation in the corporate life. For God reveals Himself objectively through the Church. That is the bedrock on which we build our faith. Our private communing with Him must have that as its foundation or it will be without adequate support. Thomas' place was with the brethren on Easter night. By absenting himself, he did not succeed in being alone with God. He failed to see the Risen Christ.

Have we not often used one or more of these excuses to justify our unwillingness to share in the life of the Christian community? Certainly, they are common enough today. "I am not good enough to go to church." "What's

the use of going. I don't get anything out of the service."
"I can find God better in the beauty of nature." We stay
away. Then some day when we want God, we discover
we do not know where to find Him. At a time when we
sorely need the support of faith, we cannot believe. The
testimony of the Church falls unconvincingly on our ears.
We have not shared in her experience. We piteously demand proof, the very proof we could have had if we had
maintained our place in the fellowship. We have wandered off to be alone—alone with our shame, alone with
our discouragement, alone with God. Suddenly we discover that we are simply—alone.

And the cure? Return to the fellowship. The Risen
Christ did not appear privately to Thomas. If it was shame
that kept him away from the others, that shame was hurt
pride. It was not penitence like that of Peter which made
him want to be with John, the disciple who knew of his
sin. Therefore, Christ did not appear to Thomas to give
him absolution. If it was discouragement that caused
Thomas to stay at home, our Lord did not lift him out of
it, as He did Mary Magdalene; since, unlike hers, his discouragement did not come from a faithful following of
his vocation. If Thomas yielded to the temptation to be
alone with God at a time when he knew the Church was
assembling, he could not, like Cleopas, plead invincible
ignorance. Of his own free will, Thomas had to abandon
his deliberate aloofness before he could be reinstated.

In spite of his inability to believe the Apostles' testimony
in regard to the Resurrection, Thomas did return to the
fellowship. Yet even this act of penitence and surrender
was not immediately rewarded with an Appearance of

the Risen Lord. Thomas had to abide with the Apostles seven days before his doubts were resolved. Thus his sincerity was tested and strengthened by perseverance. God is a loving Father. He does not spoil us by overhasty rewards. He makes us reach that we may grow. How Thomas grew through this experience will be apparent in a moment.

Growth is also the key to understanding the other alternative. Perhaps Thomas' absence was not his fault. He may have been prevented by circumstances beyond his control from being present in the Upper Room. It would be futile for us to try to guess what these circumstances might have been, since we have not the faintest clue to guide us. Nor do we have to know the nature of them. It is enough, for this present hypothesis, to assume that he was unavoidably hindered from joining the brethren.

If it was not Thomas' fault, why then did not our Lord appear to him privately? This brings us back again to that fundamental element in the spiritual life, the combat with darkness. Every soul that earnestly seeks to know and follow Christ has this experience sooner or later. To many souls, it comes again and again. There are dry patches in the prayer life when fervor is dead and God seems remote and indifferent. Doubt assails the soul and the well-springs of faith dry up. Religious exercises of all kinds degenerate into a dull and meaningless routine. It seems impossible not only to pray but to desire to pray. One keeps on going, if at all, simply by sheer force of will; and the time spent in prayer is fully occupied either in repelling distractions or in yielding to them. It may be that Thomas was called to such an experience at this time, that God allowed him to be absent in order that he might do battle with the temptation to doubt.

"Let no man say when he is tempted, I am tempted of God." The darkness and doubt did not originate in God. They came from the devil who, having captured one of the Twelve, was trying to snare another. The devil always goes after big game. Souls who have made some progress in the spiritual life must expect to be subjected to violent assaults. Those who are drifting along in a state of indifference, making little effort to respond to God, are slaves of Satan already. He is content to leave them unmolested as long as they do not realize their thraldom and struggle against it. To attack them vigorously might open their eyes and bestir them to penitence and resistance. The devil prefers to keep them bound by their habitual sins, to which they have become so accustomed that they no longer notice them. But souls who, by an earnest response to God, are escaping from Satan's control, are beset by more forceful temptations.

God allows them to be. If Thomas was absent through no fault of his own, then God permitted him to be put in a position in which he was open to attack. Does this mean that God connived with sin? Not at all. For temptation is not sin. There is nothing wicked or shameful about being tempted, provided, of course, one has not deliberately gone into the temptation when it could have been avoided. From the devil's point of view, temptation is an invitation to sin. But God intends temptation to be an occasion for victory. He never suffers us to be tempted beyond possibility of resistance, but with the temptation makes a way of escape. That is, He gives us the grace with which to resist the devil. He lets us be tempted, but we never need to yield if we use the power He makes available to us. By His strength, we can overcome evil and establish ourselves more firmly in the good.

Temptation is meant to be, as its name implies, a trial, a testing. Spiritual darkness and dryness give us a chance to remain faithful to God for His sake alone. It is easy to be true to God when everything is going smoothly, when prayer is fervent and sweet, when success crowns our efforts to serve and follow Christ. But there lurks in this situation the danger that we are being faithful in order to enjoy the benefits of God's love, rather than in order to love God Himself. Even if this was not our motive originally, it may easily become so as we get accustomed to the state of fervor, and desire to remain in it. Therefore, from time to time, God removes the emotional props, after they have fulfilled their purpose of establishing us on a certain level of the spiritual life, just as a builder removes the forms after a concrete foundation has set. This is the time of testing whether the foundation can stand by itself and support the superstructure which is about to be built on it. We must learn to persevere without having our faithfulness in prayer, in sacraments, in service rewarded by an accompanying joy. And once the foundation has set, we must press on with the work and, with God's help, build the next floor of the soul's castle upon it.

Furthermore, to change the simile, the temptation to doubt and discouragement exercises and strengthens our souls. To resist it, we must use the virtues of faith, hope, and love. The virtues are powers given to us by the Holy

Ghost. They are conferred when He comes to us in Baptism. But in order to make them our own, we must appropriate them and use them. It is not enough to eat and digest our food. If that is all we do, the food simply turns into fat. Having eaten, we must exercise. Thereby the energy derived from the food is used to build strong and healthy muscles. Our bodies are strengthened by it. What is true of our bodies is true of our souls. The power of God becomes our own only as we use it to strengthen our spiritual muscles.

We exercise the virtue of faith by using it to resist doubt. Hope is assimilated by overcoming discouragement. Love grows as we hold fast to God when we seem to be deriving no benefit from so doing. That is why God tries us from time to time by periods of dryness, doubt, and suffering. We need these times of struggle in order to develop our muscles. Without them we should remain weak and flabby souls.

Thomas is commonly called "the doubter." He might better be called "the Apostle of faith." He was beset by the temptation to doubt. In the teeth of it, he exercised the virtue of faith. He could not bring himself to believe in the Resurrection on the strength of the disciples' testimony. That was the form his temptation to doubt took. But what did he do? He returned to the fellowship of the Apostles. He could not believe what they told him; but he believed in them. He did not conclude that they were crazy or that they were liars. He did not get angry and go home to Galilee. Although he could neither understand nor share their joy, he held fast to them in the hope that sooner or later God would resolve his doubts.

Thomas did not yield to his temptation. He could not believe in the Risen Christ. But he remained faithful to the Master. He hung on to what he did know and could believe. Jesus had called him. Jesus had numbered him with the Twelve. Thomas knew that his place was among them. He knew that it was Jesus' will that he abide with them. That was his clear path of duty. He followed it. Imagine what it must have cost him. Presumably, the disciples gathered every night during Easter week. Yet our Lord did not reappear until the following Sunday. The disciples were full of joy at their knowledge of Christ's Resurrection. Thomas was prevented by his doubt from sharing in that joy. He was out of tune. While the others were praising God in exultation, Thomas sat dejectedly in their midst. They were overflowing with new life. He was conscious only of an aching void. Their efforts to convince him served but to intensify his incredulity. Their attempts to cheer him up deepened his depression. Night after night, he went to the Upper Room. Night after night, he endured the darkness, the dryness, the desolation. Night after night, he went home unsatisfied, unrelieved. But he met the test. Through all those days of suffering and spiritual combat his faith remained unshaken. He held on. He returned to the gathering of the disciples again and again. "After eight days . . . Thomas was with them: then came Jesus."

We learn from Thomas how to act in our periods of spiritual darkness. When our prayer life, such as it is, goes dead, when doubts as to this or that doctrine of the Faith attack us, when, perhaps, God and our whole relationship with Him seem suddenly to be a figment of our own imagination, when old habits of sin which we thought long since conquered rise up again and overwhelm us, when we seem entangled in a morass of sloth and lassitude, when we are discouraged and inclined to give up religion as worthless, when some suffering or disappointment comes to us and, in angry resentment, we are tempted to think that God does not love us—spiritual darkness may take many forms —then we must follow Thomas' example if we would see the Lord.

First we should ask ourselves if we have brought the darkness on ourselves. Have we been lax in our Christian duty and thereby cut ourselves off from the life of the Vine? A severed branch is dead. It must be engrafted again if it is to revive. Have we failed to repent of our sins, hiding them instead under a cloak of shame? If so, we must drag them out, face and admit them, go back to the Church and take our place among the other repentant sinners, that with them we may receive the forgiving love of God. Have we become lazy in performing our duties of prayer and worship, abandoning them because we could not see their value? Back to work at them we must go; and if, for a time, they continue to seem empty and profitless, we recognize that as a chance to show God that we are willing to perform them for His sake alone. Have we presumptuously concluded that we can get along by ourselves without the help God offers us through the Church, through the normal means of grace? Then we must return to the fellowship and take the lowest place. In time, the Master will say, "Friend, go up higher."

If, however, an honest self-appraisal does not reveal

any laxity in the performance of our spiritual duties which will account for the descent of the darkness, we should not fall into the snare of scrupulosity. We are not to go scurrying around in our souls looking for its cause. We are not to magnify insignificant failings out of all proportion and attribute it to them. Neither should we burden ourselves with a load of extra devotions in the hope that we can thereby inveigle God into restoring our lost fervor or peace of mind. Nor should we sit back and howl at heaven like a baby deprived of his rattle. We have seen that the absence from the Upper Room which precipitated Thomas' spiritual combat may not have been his fault. Likewise, our darkness may not have been caused by any failure on our part. In that case, it has been allowed to come to us in order that by remaining faithful through it we may grow and be strengthened in faith and hope and love.

Whatever the cause, the cure remains the same. Hold fast by God. Cling to Him in the ways which He has provided. This will mean regular attendance at Sunday worship, even though we find ourselves out of tune with the service and go away more depressed than ever. After all, our primary purpose in attending church is not to be entertained or uplifted, but to offer reverence and praise to God. If, because of the darkness and doubt, our hearts are too heavy for us to lift them up to God, at least we can drop them at His feet.

It will mean, also, holding fast to our routine of private devotions. Again there may be no joy, no reality, no life in them. At best, they may be a mere mechanical recitation of words. They may be the prey of constant distractions. They may seem an utter waste of time. So be it. If we can give God nothing more, let us give Him the time, no matter how heavily it hangs on our hands. If we cannot honestly tell God we love Him, let us tell Him that we want to love Him. If we do not know how to speak to Him, let us repeat quietly, "Lord, teach me to pray." If there seems to be no one to pray to, let us take on our lips the cry from the Cross and, in our Lord's spirit of humble submissive love say, "My God, my God, why hast thou forsaken me?"

The one thing needful is that we hold on to what God has already given us, our daily prayers in private and our place in the Christian fellowship. In these ways, we express our faith in action though we may not be able to believe it in our minds or feel it in our hearts. We are making the response which permits God to increase our faith. At last, He can vouchsafe us a revelation of Himself which dispels the darkness by a far greater light than we could possibly have anticipated.

When the Risen Christ came to the Upper Room the second time, with His greeting, "Peace be unto you," He at once called Thomas to Him. "Reach hither thy finger, and behold my hands; and reach hither thy hand and thrust it into my side." Thomas was invited to penetrate the Sacred Wounds. As he had suffered with Christ, he could comprehend Christ's suffering and the love which that suffering expressed. Thomas had shared to some extent the darkness of Calvary. He knew what it cost God to redeem a sinful world.

"Be not faithless, but believing." Thus our Lord conferred on Thomas the fulness of the gift of faith. Out of the struggle had come to Thomas the capacity to believe. Because he had exercised his faith in the teeth of doubt, that faith had grown mightily. Now he was in a position to outstrip his fellow-disciples. Casting himself on his knees before the Risen Christ, he cried, "My Lord and my God." He was the first to recognize and hail the Master's divinity.

Thomas was given exactly the proof he had demanded. This shows he was not wrong in asking for it. It was necessary to his vocation that he see the Risen Christ. He was called to be an Apostle, and an eye-witness of the Resurrection. His testimony is all the stronger because he was convinced in the teeth of doubt.

We are not called to be Apostles. Therefore, we must not demand that we see the Risen Christ before we believe. That is not necessary for us. The fact of the Resurrection has been abundantly well established. Christ showed Himself to many trustworthy witnesses. Their testimony has been transmitted to us through the Church, Christ's own Body through which He speaks to every age. It has been recorded for us in the Spirit-inspired Scriptures. In recent years, the evidence has been sifted by every device of modern scholarship and has stood the test. It is a sure foundation on which we can build our faith. We need not and we must not ask for any other.

We are eligible for a blessing which Thomas himself could not receive. As our Lord pointed out to him at the time, in order to protect him from spiritual pride, there was a limitation to his faith. It was confirmed only by seeing the Risen Christ. "Thomas, because thou hast seen me, thou hast believed." That was a high calling and a great privilege. Yet there is a greater which may be ours, if, like Thomas, we are faithful to the light that has been granted us, if, in times of doubt and darkness, we hold fast to Christ in the fellowship of His Church. "Blessed are they that have not seen, and yet have believed." As Thomas emerged from his spiritual combat to outstrip his fellow-disciples, so we can outstrip him. We may walk by faith and not by sight even through the valley of the shadow of death, fearing no evil, for we know that Christ is with us, that His rod and His staff comfort us.

IX

God's Little Ones

*After that, he was seen of above five hundred brethren at once;
of whom the greater part remain unto this present, but some
are fallen asleep.*

I CORINTHIANS 15:6.

The Appearance to the five hundred brethren presumably took place in Galilee. Our Lord probably did not have that many disciples in Jerusalem except at the time of the great feasts. Galilee was the scene of His ministry and there the majority of His disciples lived. Often He had drawn crowds into the hills that He might preach to them. Now He called them forth again that He might appear to them in His Risen Body.

This meeting must have been the result of definite planning. Five hundred brethren would not just happen to be in the same place at the same time. They were gathered to meet the Lord. Perhaps we get the first step in the preparation for this Appearance in the message of the angel to the women at the tomb. "Tell his disciples and Peter that he goeth before you into Galilee: there shall ye see him." More specific directions may have been given by our Lord at the Appearances in the Upper Room.

Shortly after the second of these Appearances, the Apostles set out for Galilee. Arriving there, they proceeded to pass through the villages, calling the faithful to the place of meeting. Thither from all directions they journeyed, men, women, children, carrying their provisions with them, sleeping in the open fields.

It was a large crowd. St. Paul says it numbered "above five hundred brethren." Since he is listing the official witnesses of the Resurrection, the number may refer only to the men present. That seems to have been common practice. The figure for the multitude who were fed with the loaves and fishes is given by St. Matthew as "about five thousand men, beside women and children." The latter were certainly present at the Resurrection Appearance. If we should add them to the number given, that brings the total up to over a thousand.

The reference to the feeding of the multitude reminds us, however, that the crowd assembled for the Resurrection Appearance was only one-tenth the size of that gathered on the former occasion. Already the scandal of the Cross was beginning to operate—"unto the Jews a stumblingblock." People flocked to our Lord to hear Him preach and to receive the Bread from Heaven. But as soon as the cause was officially discredited, as soon as the threat of persecution arose, as soon as the report of the Resurrection put demands on faith, all but a remnant fell away. It is still true today. Crowded churches mean little, unless those who fill them have faced the Cross and accepted the Resurrection.

The faithful remnant was the group through whom God had to give Himself to the world, for they alone would receive Him. The continuity of Jewish history was preserved through the remnant. The majority of the people always followed their selfish impulses into the oblivion of self-destruction. The Prophets were scorned and scoffed at by the multitudes. A handful of disciples rallied about them and wrote down their words, passing them on to future generations. The people at large accepted and revered the Prophets only after their message no longer had an immediate reference to contemporary events and hence could be reduced to pious platitudes.

After the Exile, a remnant returned to the Holy Land. Not only were the ten tribes who were carried off by the Assyrians completely absorbed into their new environment. Many of those who were taken to Babylon were lost through the same process; and of the remainder who were loyal to Jehovah and the Law, few were willing to return with Zerubbabel, Nehemiah, and Ezra. Those who went back in the first migration were almost swallowed up by the inhabitants of the land who had moved in during the Babylonian Captivity. Even after they were strengthened by subsequent migrations, it took the full efforts of the leaders and of the truly faithful Jews to carry out the plan of rebuilding the Temple and to prevent the intermingling of the Jews with their Gentile neighbors.

Again, when Antiochus Epiphanes tried to Hellenize the Palestinian Jews, resistance came solely from the faithful remnant. They formed the backbone of the Maccabean movement. When success diverted this from its original religious purpose to a quest for mere national aggrandizement, the remnant detached itself from it, continued to concentrate on the observance of the Law, and fostered the hope of the imminent advent of the Messiah.

Consequently, this was the group which was prepared

to receive Him. We meet them on every page of the New
Testament. Zacharias and Elizabeth "were both righteous
before God, walking in all the commandments and ordi-
nances of the Lord blameless." They were called to be the
parents of the Forerunner, John the Baptist, through whom
the moral zeal and messianic hope became vocal in
prophecy. St. Joseph must be numbered in this faithful
remnant, as must Saints Joachim and Anne, if those are the
names of the parents of the Virgin Mary. She herself is
the supreme figure of the group; her purity and her consent made the Incarnation possible. Others of whom we
think are Simeon and Anna who welcomed the Messiah
in the temple; and the twelve Apostles and the holy women,
many of whom had previously been disciples of John the
Baptist.

These were the outstanding persons whose vocation to an
important rôle in our Lord's ministry has preserved their
names for us. We get glimpses of others in the background.
There were the shepherds watching their flocks by night
who were invited to Bethlehem to worship the infant
Redeemer. There were the seventy whom our Lord sent
out two by two "into every city and place, whither he
himself would come." There were the various persons who
approached our Lord for help and advice during His ministry. Finally, five hundred of them went out to an appointed place in the Galilean hills to see the Risen Christ.

Who were they? Not the official leaders of Judaism,
neither the Pharisees, the religious rulers, nor the Herodians,
the civil authorities. Not, for the most part, the wealthy
or the prominent. They were poor, humble folk, farm-
laborers, shepherds and fishermen, with a scattering of

local artisans who, in spite of their special trades, were little differentiated from their unskilled brethren. Accompanying them were their wives and daughters, hard-working peasant women, accustomed to a dawn-to-sunset round of daily tasks. And darting here and there among their slow-footed elders were the inevitable children, ragged, dirty, and disheveled, but introducing a carefree note into the expedition.

A Roman centurion would have laughed at this first legion of the army of Christ. "Rabble" is the epithet which would have suggested itself to his mind, save that its connotations of potential destructive danger are too strong. One look at their careworn faces, their toil-gnarled hands, their bodies emaciated by the meager living which was all they could wrest from the stubborn earth, and he would have turned away with a shrug of his shoulders—unless he happened to notice the light of faith in their eyes.

These were the spiritual forefathers of the movement which was to bring the haughty Roman Empire to its knees in homage to God, which was to survive its collapse and convert its barbarian conquerors, which was to build up its own civilization and to outlast its disintegration through internecine strife, which was, even when rent by internal dissensions, to fling its missions to the four corners of the earth. These were, in short, the vanguard of the Christian Church, the Body of the living God. They were chosen because they alone would heed His call—the weak, the poor, the disenfranchised, the oppressed, but those who heard the word of God and kept it. Jesus reveled in their lowliness. "I thank thee, O Father, Lord of heaven and earth, that thou hast hid these things from the wise and prudent, and hast revealed them unto babes."

"Blessed be ye poor, for yours is the kingdom of God. Blessed are ye that hunger now. . . . blessed are ye that weep now. . . . blessed are ye, when men shall hate you." Why are these the people among whom the Gospel finds its most eager adherents? Not just because they are poor, undernourished, overburdened, and oppressed. Only five hundred of all the poverty-stricken men of Galilee went out to see the Lord. Poverty, tyranny, and inadequate standards of living are not good but evil. All those who have to endure them are not thereby made spiritually receptive. Many are hardened by them, provoked to crime and rebellion. Yet others by the same school of suffering are turned into saints. Others still, who had great possessions, have, at the call of Christ, either divested themselves of them altogether, or possessed them "as though they possessed not," counting it a privilege to share the hardships of the destitute.

What constitutes the difference? "Blessed are the poor in spirit." Scholars tell us that the words "in spirit" cannot be translated back into Aramaic, the language which our Lord spoke. Hence they were not in the beatitude when He pronounced it. They are an editorial comment by the first Evangelist, introduced to bring out the technical significance of the word "poor" as our Lord used it. He spoke of those who were content to be poor, who asked no more of this world's goods than a bare living and a chance, in small but personal ways, to alleviate the sufferings of others—yes, who were content to put up with less than that if the only alternatives were revolt, crime, or the absorption of all their energies in scheming ambition. The motive for this submission is not, of course, indolence or a spineless acquiescence in injustice. It is the recognition that our true treasure is in heaven and that the laying up of it should be the chief concern of our sojourn on earth. It is not lack of possessions which nurtures sanctity, but the reduction of our material needs to their simplest terms in order that time and energy may be devoted to the pursuit of eternal values. It is not lack of ambition, but ambition for the things of God.

Other-worldliness is fundamental to Christianity. No one can seek, let alone obtain, the full benefits of the spiritual life unless he curtails his desires for earthly possessions and comforts. Never was the recognition of this truth more difficult than it is today. The basis of our economic theory is mass production, which brings with it the necessity of increasing the market by stimulating in people a sense of need for things which otherwise it would never occur to them to want. In so far as this applies our recent technological advances to a genuine enrichment of our lives, providing better living standards, labor- and time-saving devices, and wholesome cultural and recreational opportunities, it is all to the good. But when it creates a desire for things of no intrinsic value, which nobody really wants, when it encourages people to devote all their energies to the struggle to obtain them, when it focuses our attention solely on "What shall we eat?" or, "What shall we drink?" or, "Wherewithal shall we be clothed?"—then it is in direct conflict with the teaching of Christ.

We cannot serve God and mammon. Not only is there

insufficient time and energy for an all-out quest of both
material and spiritual values; the mere possession of super-
fluous creature comforts, or an unrestrained desire for them,
produces a condition of soul which is not conducive to
spiritual growth. The indulgence of our appetites increases
their demands and lessens the control of our wills over
them. Mortification, self-denial, and self-discipline are essential to healthy personalities. These can, to some extent,
be imposed upon ourselves, but only if we resist with
unflagging determination the appeal of modern advertis-
ing. Far more effective, however, is the discipline imposed
from without, the lack of funds with which to satisfy
all our desires, the need for hard work to provide a living,
and the patient endurance of privation and suffering, of
injustice and persecution when necessary. If these things
are accepted with glad hearts, because we realize that we
can give up all material and earthly values for God and be
the richer by the exchange, then they speed us on our way
to Him. We learn to be poor in spirit, that ours may be
the Kingdom of heaven.

"A slave morality," was Nietzsche's indictment of Christianity. "An opiate of the people," charges the social
reformer who claims that the hope of eternal life is cultivated in order to distract us from our present misery.
"An escape from reality," adds the materialist psychologist
whose ideal for the normal man is an efficient quest for
wealth. But suppose Christianity is true. Suppose God is
the Ultimate Reality. Then those who are absorbed in
seeking transitory things are the escapists. Suppose our joy
is to be found only in God. Then those whose hopes and

ideals are earthbound are chasing shadows. Suppose that by becoming slaves to Christ we are made sons of God.

The five hundred Galilean peasants with their wives and children saw the Lord. They shared the Apostolic vocation. Christianity is not a religion of the élite. Its highest privileges are open to its humblest members. Its Gospel rests on certain facts of history: a Child was born in Bethlehem during the reign of Herod the Great; a Man was crucified under Pontius Pilate on Calvary Hill and subsequently was seen, risen from the dead, in Jerusalem and Galilee. These events are interpreted by a few doctrines, summarized in the Creeds—doctrines so simple that a child may learn them, yet so profound that the greatest theologians cannot exhaust their meaning. This teaching is made available through the Church which speaks with the authority of God Himself. The power to live in the light of these truths and to know the Risen Lord is conveyed in definite, objective ways through the sacraments.

That is all; yet it is enough. By it, souls with little intellectual capacity, with no outstanding talents whatever, have been raised to the heights of sanctity. On the other hand, those who have come bearing great gifts, profound minds, creative artistic ability, loving hearts, pure souls, if they placed them at the feet of Christ, have found them fully employed by Him. "High and low, rich and poor, one with another," they find in Christ their complete satisfaction and their everlasting reward.

The majority will always be poor, humble folk. There were twelve Apostles and five hundred brethren. Even the Apostles were drawn from the same peasant stock. So it was to remain. St. Paul points out the fitness and the significance of this. "For ye see your calling, brethren, how that not many wise men after the flesh, not many mighty, not many noble, are called: but God hath chosen the foolish things of the world to confound the wise; and God hath chosen the weak things of the world to confound the things which are mighty; and base things of the world, and things which are despised, hath God chosen, yea, and things which are not, to bring to nought things that are: that no flesh should glory in His presence." God has a special tenderness in His love for the little ones of the earth. They give themselves to Him with wholehearted devotion; He may lavish on them His gifts without fear that they will be tempted to pride, and He can manifest His power the more gloriously through their weakness.

St. Paul lists five witnesses or groups of witnesses of the Resurrection besides himself. Only to one group does he seem to refer his readers for verification. This is the five hundred brethren, "of whom," he says, "the greater part remain unto this present, but some are fallen asleep." He recognized the value of their testimony.

At first this may seem strange. Few of the five hundred were missionaries as we think of the term. After seeing the Lord they returned to their farms, their flocks, their fishing-nets. They did not preach. They did not carry the Gospel to foreign lands. They went right on being Galilean peasants engaged in their lowly tasks. How was their witness given, and why was it important?

Theirs was a living testimony. They did not have to speak much of the Risen Christ. The light of His glory shone forth from their eyes. He was the center of their lives. Not only did they worship Him in the Breaking of Bread and prayers; they worked for Him, doing everything with a care that made it a worthy offering. They took Him into their homes, patterning the relationships between husband and wife, between parents and children on His love for them. They served Him in the least of their brethren. They lived the Christian Life.

Theirs was also a corporate witness. At first, in each village, they formed a group within the synagog, distinguished by their devotion, by their claim that Jesus was the Messiah, and by their weekly commemoration of the Resurrection on Sunday in addition to the Sabbath observances. Eventually, when the tension between Jews and Christians increased, they were expelled from the synagogs and formed their own. Always they manifested a high degree of fraternal charity. For a while, they had all things in common. When that was found no longer feasible, they continued to share their wealth, such as it was, with each other, to care for and to comfort the needy, and to hold together in the closest bonds of brotherhood. Even their enemies were forced to exclaim, "How the Christians love one another."

This is the basic form of Christian witness—the establishment in the midst of a sinful world of a God-centered society. If the Church is not winning the world as it should today, the reason is that the average Christian has forgotten his missionary vocation. All too often he thinks of religion as something he does on Sunday (if he feels like it), as something designed to help him. He neither enters wholeheartedly into the life of the fellowship nor feels any obligation to share it with others. Instead of drawing men to Christ, he keeps them away.

"He that gathereth not with me scattereth." That is the scandal of these times. The worldling looks at the average congregation, riddled with petty feuds, jealousy, and gossip, and says, "If that is Christian fellowship, I will have none of it." Or he looks at individual Christians striving selfishly for material gain, casually committing the whole gamut of sin, and says, "Why should I be a Christian? Christians are no better than anyone else." Thus we who call ourselves by Christ's name, crucify to ourselves the Son of God afresh and put Him to an open shame.

It need not be. Like the five hundred brethren, we can go forth, Sunday by Sunday, to take our place in the fellowship and see the Lord—not in His Risen Body, but in His Body the Church. Empowered by Him, we can go back into the world and show forth His joy and love in our daily lives. We may be very little people, with few talents, engaged in humdrum tasks. But if we put on the Lord Jesus Christ and make not provision for the flesh to fulfil the lusts thereof, He will manifest His almighty power through our weakness. We shall become living witnesses drawing men to Him.

X

The Way of the Cross

*After these things Jesus shewed himself again to the disciples
at the sea of Tiberias; and on this wise shewed he himself. There
were together Simon Peter, and Thomas called Didymus, and
Nathanael of Cana in Galilee, and the sons of Zebedee, and two
other of His disciples. Simon Peter saith unto them, I go a fishing. They say unto him, We also go with thee. They went
forth, and entered into a ship immediately; and that night they
caught nothing. But when morning was now come, Jesus stood
on the shore: but the disciples knew not that it was Jesus. Then
Jesus saith unto them, Children, have ye any meat? They answered him, No. And he said unto them, Cast the net on the
right side of the ship, and ye shall find. They cast therefore,
and now they were not able to draw it for the multitude of
fishes. Therefore that disciple whom Jesus loved saith unto Peter,
It is the Lord. Now when Simon Peter heard that it was the
Lord, he girt his fisher's coat unto him, (for he was naked,)
and did cast himself into the sea. And the other disciples came
in a little ship; (for they were not far from land, but as it
were two hundred cubits,) dragging the net with fishes. As
soon then as they were come to land, they saw a fire of coals
there, and fish laid thereon, and bread. Jesus saith unto them,
Bring of the fish which ye have now caught. Simon Peter went
up, and drew the net to land full of great fishes, an hundred
and fifty and three: and for all there were so many, yet was
not the net broken. Jesus saith unto them, Come and dine.
And none of the disciples durst ask him, Who art thou? knowing that it was the Lord. Jesus then cometh, and taketh bread,
and giveth them, and fish likewise. This is now the third time
that Jesus shewed himself to his disciples, after that he was*

risen from the dead. So when they had dined, Jesus saith to
Simon Peter, Simon, son of Jonas, lovest thou me more than
these? He saith unto him, Yea, Lord; thou knowest that I love
thee. He saith unto him, Feed my lambs. He saith to him again
the second time, Simon, son of Jonas, lovest thou me? He saith
unto him, Yea, Lord; thou knowest that I love thee. He saith
unto him, Feed my sheep. He saith unto him the third time,
Simon, son of Jonas, lovest thou me? Peter was grieved because
he said unto him the third time, Lovest thou me? And he said
unto him, Lord, thou knowest all things; thou knowest that I
love thee. Jesus saith unto him, Feed my sheep. Verily, verily, I
say unto thee, When thou wast young, thou girdedest thyself, and
walkedst wither thou wouldest: but when thou shalt be old, thou
shalt stretch forth thy hands, and another shall gird thee, and
carry thee whither thou wouldest not. This spake he, signifying
by what death he should glorify God. And when he had spoken
this, he saith unto him, Follow me. Then Peter, turning about,
seeth the disciple whom Jesus loved following; which also leaned
on his breast at supper, and said, Lord, which is he that betrayeth
thee? Peter seeing him saith to Jesus, Lord, and what shall this
man do? Jesus saith unto him, If I will that he tarry till I
come, what is that to thee? follow thou me.

ST. JOHN 21:1-22.

"I go a fishing." Does it seem strange that Peter and
his companions should have decided to return to their
former trade after all that had happened? If we think
so, we have failed to grasp their point of view. Contact
with the Risen Christ did not give them a sense of their
own importance. They did not consider that their experience had lifted them out of their old social status. They
knew they were called to witness to the Resurrection. But
as yet they had not received the commission and command

to go "into all the world, and preach the Gospel to every creature." They assumed, therefore, that they were to return to their own villages and, like the rest of the five hundred brethren, bear their testimony in terms of daily living.

They were fishermen. Jesus had called them from their nets to accompany Him in His public ministry. Now He had laid down His life and taken it up again. They recognized Him as Lord and Christ. They would serve Him for the rest of their lives. How better could they serve Him than by plying the trade of fishing at which they were experts? They would do the job to the best of their ability and manifest in it the new power and love and joy which they had received from the Risen Lord.

We know that our Lord had other plans for them. They were to be "fishers of men." After Pentecost, they would be too busy winning souls and organizing the infant Christian community to spend much time on the Lake of Galilee. Eventually, they would be sent forth from Palestine to carry the Gospel to foreign lands. All that, however, was in the future, still hidden from their eyes. It would be revealed to them when the time came. They did not take it upon themselves either to plan or to anticipate such a career. The height of their ambition was to be good, hard-working fishermen. They believed that to be the means by which they could best give glory to God and help to their fellow-men.

This humility on their part was not displeasing to Christ. It was just the material He needed for His work. His Appearance to them while they were thus engaged shows that He approved their decision to go fishing. That was their vocation at the moment. The opening part of the episode we are considering shows Christ's interest in its success.

"Children, have ye any meat?" was His greeting to them. Peering across the lake hag-ridden by the morning mists, they failed to recognize Him. They called back, "No." Their night's toil had yielded them nothing. "Cast the net on the right side of the ship, and ye shall find." They did as He commanded. When they drew it up again, the net was full of fishes. John whispered, "It is the Lord," and Peter cast himself into the sea in his haste to greet the Master.

The others got the nets to land. There they discovered that not only had Christ given them a mammoth draught, but also had provided a fire and bread, and a fish was baking on the coals. At His command, they added another from the catch and sat down to dine with Him. It was like the old times before the Crucifixion. But the ordinariness of the outward scene heightened their sense of awe. In this common, familiar setting they communed with the Risen Christ. Along with the joy at His presence there was a note of reverence, restraint, even embarrassment. "None . . . durst ask Him, Who art thou? knowing that it was the Lord."

We need this episode to help us grasp the full significance of the Resurrection. It brings us down to earth. Here we see the Risen Christ concerning Himself with the physical comfort of His disciples and prospering them in their labors as fishermen. This reminds us that God is not interested solely in what we call spiritual things. He created the whole of our nature—body, mind, and soul. He desires the welfare of our whole being. He wants our bodies fed and clothed, our minds trained and educated, our hearts gladdened by beauty and laughter, as well as our souls redeemed and nourished. Religion is concerned with every department of life. Anything that ministers to human needs is the service of God in the brethren.

This reminder is timely today. We have over-spiritualized religion. We limit it to our relationship with God in terms of prayer, worship, and morality. The concept of vocation is still unduly restricted. A few years ago, we spoke of vocation only in connection with those called to the active ministry of the Church. Recently, we have grown a bit wiser. Nowadays, we include certain of the professions—medicine, law, teaching, social work—those that aim directly at the betterment of human society. But we rarely go beyond that. We find it hard to believe that God is interested in such mundane matters as banking and manufacture, as mining and farming, or in such frivolities as entertainment and amusement, as sports and dancing. We seldom speak of His calling men and women to be stenographers and bookkeepers, machinists or day-laborers, farmhands or cattle-ranchers, firemen or street-cleaners, salesgirls or housewives, artists or radio comedians.

Yet He does. These are all jobs that He wants done to provide us with the necessities and the joys of life. He calls the majority of men and women to serve Him in such occupations. By them, they are not only to earn a living. They are to share in God's work, act as His hands and feet, conferring on mankind the benefits He wills to bestow. He has His standards for them to attain. To fulfil these vocations it is not enough to get by, to satisfy the boss, to hold one's job, to make money. The work should be done with such care and diligence as to make it a worthy offering to Him who said, "Ye shall be holy: for I the Lord your God am holy."

The substitution of the profit motive for the sense of vocation as the stimulus to work is the modern tragedy. Business has degenerated into a sordid quest for gain; industry is torn by the selfish strife between the rival interests of management and labor; agriculture is the victim alternately of mortgage foreclosures and of government subsidy; cheap and shoddy goods are dumped on a gullible public; art and professional entertainment have been debauched by the profitable catering to a depraved public taste. Every so often, the pressure of this accumulated selfishness explodes into war.

How strange it is that Christians should have forgotten that all honest work is meant to be the means of serving God! For Christ Himself was a Carpenter. That was His vocation until He was "about thirty years of age." Let us not understate the significance of this. Christ did not merely condescend to demonstrate the dignity of labor by working at a carpenter's bench while He was waiting for the time to come when He would begin His real vocation. He was called to be the village Carpenter of Nazareth. That was just as truly the work His Father gave Him to do as His subsequent preaching, miracles, and death on the cross. The fashioning of plows and yokes, the mending of children's toys, the turning out of wooden drinking bowls for the local marriage feasts were integral parts of His service of God. He did them all with the same spirit of obedience and devotion, of patience and courtesy, which we find displayed in His public ministry. His hammer, His saw, and His plane were, like His cross and His crown of thorns, tools that He used to redeem the world. For He was not only the Good Shepherd who laid down His life for His sheep; He was also the Good Workman who sanctified His trade.

When He appeared to His disciples at the end of their night's work, He first made their labors fruitful and gave them a hearty breakfast. He knew that hungry and dis- couraged men are not in a condition to rise up to spiritual things. Accordingly He wants Christians to continue His work of satisfying men's physical needs and of giving them good cheer, in order that they may be able to serve Him in their several callings with strong bodies, sound minds, and glad hearts.

This is the background against which Christ indicated to two of His disciples the further development of their vocations. He turned first to Peter. We have already seen how He had hastened to meet Peter's penitence with His loving pardon. That, however, was a private transaction. It caught Peter up once more into the full experience of the Master's personal love. Now Peter was to be given an opportunity to make reparation for his threefold denial by a threefold declaration of love, and thereby publicly to be reinstated to his place as leader of the Apostles.

"Simon, son of Jonas, lovest thou me more than these?" Peter's response to this question thrice repeated is a fas- cinating study in character, if we remember to whom our Lord was speaking. It was to the impetuous Simon Peter —and he was not one whit less impetuous than he had been before. About an hour earlier he had leapt out of the ship into the sea, as soon as he recognized Christ, because he was in such a hurry to greet Him. He could not wait for the boats to be beached even though "they were not far from land, but as it were two hundred cubits." Peter was always to retain his impetuosity; it was part of his natural endowment, a consequence of his zeal. Conversion and penitence were not to diminish that. Grace does not override nature; it consecrates it.

We see this happening in Peter's answers. At the Last Supper, when Peter's love was questioned, his impetuous zeal replied with a boast, "Lord, I am ready to go with thee, both into prison, and to death." With supreme self-confidence he offered to prove his love. Now, on the shore of the Lake of Galilee, the Master's questions brought before Peter's eyes that scene in the High Priest's courtyard, which effectively silenced any impulse to boast. Thus penitence wrought its work. Peter, no less zealous, no less loving, had learned the art of self-distrust. He could offer nothing to demonstrate His love. He had to trust in the Master's knowledge of his heart. "Yea, Lord; thou knowest that I love thee."

Peter could not be shaken from his humble submission. Once, twice, three times, "Lovest thou me?" "Peter was grieved because he said unto him the third time, Lovest thou me?" Even though the thought, "He does not believe me," must have flashed into Peter's mind, he did not yield to the temptation to boast or to prove his love. He deliberately rejected the idea that our Lord could be doubting him. "Lord, thou knowest all things; thou knowest that I love thee."

Each of Peter's professions of love was greeted by a command, "Feed my lambs. . . . Feed my sheep." Out of Peter's penitence our Lord had drawn a humility which equipped Peter for his work as pastor of souls. For the flock of Christ was to be fed with Christ, not with Peter. Only when Peter had learned to count himself nothing, to trust entirely to the knowledge, the power, the love of our Lord, was he fit to minister to the brethren the manifold riches of God. Thus we see the growth of Peter's love. Out of self-knowledge, penitence. Out of penitence, humility. Out of humility, service.

And after service, sacrifice. "When thou wast young, thou girdedest thyself, and walkedest whither thou wouldest," our Lord reminded him. The headstrong Peter—it was not so long since he had "put away childish things." "But," Christ went on to predict, "when thou shalt be old, thou shalt stretch forth thy hands, and another shall gird thee, and carry thee whither thou wouldest not." "This spake he," comments St. John, "signifying by what death he should glorify God." Tradition says that he was crucified and that, at his own request—impetuous to the last, but now impetuous in his humility—he was nailed to the cross upside down as a fitting differentiation from his Master.

The successful Christian life runs uphill—up the hill of Calvary. The realization of this often comes as a shock to beginners. They have laboriously climbed over the first hurdle of penitence. They have begun to master the first principles of prayer. They are ambitious to serve God. Now, they think, all will be smooth sailing. But God has a greater favor in store for us than that. As we grow more generous with Him, He lets us share more and more of His work in the world. We begin by participating in the work of His hidden years at Nazareth—by doing our job well, whatever it may be. We go on to the activities of His public ministry—feeding the hungry, comforting the afflicted, showing others the way to God. Then He gives us the greatest privilege of all—that of joining Him on the Cross.

Christ came to redeem the world. This could not be effected merely by teaching men what God is like and what they ought to do. To a greater or less extent we know these things already; at least we know far more than we practice. We fall short of our ideals, inadequate though these ideals may be. "The good that I would I do not: but the evil which I would not, that I do." Our Lord's work of revelation had to be supplemented by the power to follow it, if it was to benefit mankind.

The first step toward releasing that power was to free man from the shackles that bound him. The hold of evil on man's heart had to be broken. Our Lord could not do this by the patchwork methods of healing a person here and there, of casting out a few demons. These were only the opening skirmishes in His struggle with the forces of evil. They dealt with their effects, not their cause. To win man's redemption, Christ had to meet the devil face to face in mortal combat. That duel was fought on Calvary. The devil chose the weapons—suffering. By tempting human beings into sin, he induced them to heap pain, ignominy, defeat, and death on God Incarnate. In this way, the devil hoped to provoke Jesus into giving up His attempt to save man, or at least so to discredit Him in man's eyes that His efforts would bear no fruit.

Our Lord laid hold on the same weapon—suffering. He made it the supreme expression of His love. Without murmur, without complaint, without protest, He bore all the torture, physical, mental, and spiritual, that was heaped upon Him. Never once did He answer sin with sin. He always answered with love. "Father, forgive them; for they know not what they do." Never once did He let darkness engender despair. "My God, my God," He cried, speaking to the Father whom He knew to be at hand even when the desolation forced Him to ask, "Why hast thou forsaken me?" Never once did apparent failure make Him think the cause was lost. "It is finished," He shouted triumphantly at the moment when things looked blackest. Never once did He quail before the approach of death. "Father, into thy hands I commend my spirit."

That was the victory of Calvary—love conquering evil, hate, and sin by humble, patient suffering. That was the sacrifice which redeemed the world and opened to us the path to God. But Christ did not do all our suffering for us. He loves us too much for that. He bore the brunt of it. He bore what we could not. He won the decisive battle. Now He wants to repeat His victory in and through us and let us share in it.

This is done by His conquering sin and evil in us with the same weapon He used on Calvary. There are two aspects of the battle. One is the conquest of our own sin, by penitence which repudiates our past offenses and allows God to forgive them, and by self-discipline and mortification which root out our habitual weaknesses to temptation. The other is the conquest of evil in the world in which we live. Here the technique as well as the weapon is that of Calvary. Evil attacks us in the form of other people's sins. We answer with forgiveness. "Till seven times?" "I say not unto thee, Until seven times: but, Until seventy times seven." Evil attacks in the form of temptation. We beat it down, by the power of Christ, being obedient to God, if necessary, "unto death, even the death of the Cross." Evil attacks by smashing our most cherished plans. From Calvary we draw the strength to believe that failure can be, in the hands of God, the surest way of redeeming the world.

It is a mighty privilege to be cross-bearers with Christ. For each of us God has designed a cross suited to our individual needs. No two crosses are exactly alike. The Risen Christ pointed this out to Peter in answer to the latter's question concerning John, "Lord, and what shall this man do?" The Master answered, "If I will that he tarry till I come, what is that to thee? follow thou me." John was to have his cross—but it was not to be the same as Peter's. Peter's job was to carry his own.

John's cross was no less heavy. It involved much physical suffering. If the tradition that he was boiled in oil at Rome is correct, then he experienced all of martyrdom except the release of death. Instead, he was sent to Patmos to work as a slave in the mines. Finally, he was set free and went to Ephesus where the burdens of the Church fell on his aged shoulders. The full weight of John's cross, however, did not lie in any of this. What John felt most keenly was his separation from his Beloved. Of course, John was in the closest communion with Christ that is possible through prayer and sacraments; but, at best, in this life "we see through a glass, darkly" and not face to face. To the ardent lover, this was all the difference between exile and home.

One after another the Apostles died and took their places at the Marriage Feast of the Lamb. John tarried on, engaged in lowly kitchen tasks. He accepted his cross. He threw himself wholeheartedly into his daily work, for it was the offering his Beloved asked him to make. But his heart longed for the moment when he could depart and be with Christ. When, at the end of the Revelation vouchsafed him on Patmos, our Lord said to John, "Surely I come quickly," John answered, "Even so, come, Lord Jesus." Yet John had still ten years more to wait.

This tarrying purified John's love. We have seen how his hot-headedness, which won him the nickname "son of thunder," was rebuked during our Lord's public ministry. After the Ascension, his love was filtered through a long period of tarrying until it became the sparkling river that runs through his Gospel and Epistles. Thus the Beloved Disciple became the Apostle of love.

Our cross will transform us in the same way. It is designed to purge away the dross of our selfishness. It is our opportunity to be used by Christ in the conquest of evil, to share in His redemptive work. Our cross comes to us now in terms of the dull hard work to which our present vocation calls us, in terms of the aches and pains, the handicaps and disappointments, the injuries and misunderstandings which we are asked to bear. That is our cross. We must not ask or seek another. We must accept and bear it gladly. If we do, we shall find it the ladder by which we can scale the heights of heaven. There is no other way. "Whosoever doth not bear his cross, and come after me, cannot be my disciple."

XI

The Virgin Mother

Blessed are the pure in heart: for they shall see God.
ST. MATTHEW 5:8.

In this chapter, we frankly enter the realm of speculation. There is no account or reference in the Gospel to the
Appearances which we shall consider. Yet we are confident
that our Lord must have appeared to His Mother. We can
be reasonably certain that she was present at the Appearances in the Upper Room. St. Luke tells us that the Apostles
were gathered there, "and them that were with them." We
know that Mary was with them in the sense that she was
living in the home of the Beloved Disciple, to whose care our
Lord had committed her on Calvary. It is hard to believe
that she was left at John's house when the Church was
gathering in the Upper Room. She may well have been
among the five hundred in Galilee. She probably was at
Bethany when Christ ascended into heaven. We know that
she was with the Church in the Upper Room during the
days after the Ascension, for she is mentioned by name.

We are thinking here, however, not of her participation
in these public occasions, but of our Lord's private Appearances to her. Her relationship to Him assures us that these
must have taken place. She was His Mother. What loving
son would fail to visit his mother, or would be content to

see her only as one of a crowd? Would he not seek her out and commune with her alone? Would Christ the perfect Son display less filial love than this?

Perhaps some might feel this is introducing too sentimental a note. That objection misses the whole point of the Resurrection. Our Lord rose from the dead as a Man. As a Man, He is Mary's Son. His human relationships and the duties and loves which they entail persist through death. Only because this is true can we hope to be reunited with our loved ones who have gone before or whom we leave behind when our time comes. Heaven would be a poorer place were we not to find there a closer intimacy with our parents, our husbands or wives, our children, our brothers and sisters. Those loves can be very wonderful on earth; yet here there is always some sense of incompleteness in the union. In heaven, we shall all be one, even as God is One.

"Honour thy father and thy mother" is a commandment of God's law which our Lord fulfilled. During the forty days of Eastertide, the highest honor Christ had to bestow was an Appearance in His Risen Body. Would He not have honored His Mother by appearing just to her, not once but many times, spending quiet hours in loving intimacy with her whom, among all human beings, He held most dear?

Some have felt that His love and His desire to give her primary honor would have led our Lord to appear first to her. They have suggested that He went to her before He showed Himself to Mary Magdalene. Perhaps. But is it not a higher honor that He should have waited, and demonstrated His trust in her faith? Those early Appearances to individuals, as we have seen, were designed to prepare their recipients to take their places in the Upper Room for the first official Appearance. Their confusion, their need for assurance prompted Christ to show Himself to them. He did not appear to the eight disciples whose loyalty to the fellowship was sufficient to take them to the place of meeting without further assistance; nor to John, who saw the Empty Tomb and believed. By the same token it was not necessary for Christ to appear to Mary. She was perfectly attuned to her divine Son. Should we deny her the greater honor of assuming that her faith surpassed even that of John? Would she not on Calvary itself have sensed the joy that was set before Christ in the strength of which He "endured the cross, despising the shame"? Dare we not suggest that even then she anticipated His Resurrection, that she believed throughout the period when His Body lay in the grave? It is significant that she did not join the holy women in their visit to the sepulchre.

The Church has never hesitated to give to the Virgin Mary the highest honor compatible with the fact that she is a creature. It has not, of course, worshiped her as God. She is a human being and no more than a human being. But she is "our tainted nature's solitary boast."[1] Throughout her life, she was always perfectly responsive to the divine will. She was without sin. This was necessary to her vocation as the Mother of God. She was given the power to remain sinless. Of her own free will, she used the power and fulfilled her vocation.

To honor Mary does not detract in the slightest degree from the honor due to Christ. Indeed, because we reverence Christ, we revere her. When we respect someone, we always honor those whom he loves, and especially his mother.

[1] Wordsworth, *Ecclesiastical Sonnets.*

Furthermore, the holiness we salute in Mary is the work of Christ. She was full of grace, or, as the King James Version translates it, "highly favoured." This phrase underlines for us the truth that grace is a favor, an undeserved gift of Christ. Mary was freed from the taint of original sin. That simply means that she received the grace of Baptism in anticipation. She was given the fulness of the divine power with which to remain faithful to God. These benefits were made available to her because of the relationship to Christ to which she was called, because of her part in His work of salvation. Mary, like all other human souls who correspond with the redemption wrought by Christ, was saved by His merits. It is His handiwork that we honor when we respect the perfection of Mary.

Yet because she was a free agent she deserves our admiration and gratitude in her own right as well. Her faithfulness to the grace which was given her made the Incarnation possible. In all the choices of her early life she retained her purity and sanctity. Finally, the Angel Gabriel was sent to her. "Fear not, Mary: for thou hast found favour with God. And, behold, thou shalt conceive in thy womb, and bring forth a Son, and shalt call his name Jesus. He shall be great, and shall be called the Son of the Highest: and the Lord God shall give unto him the throne of his father David: and he shall reign over the house of Jacob for ever; and of his Kingdom there shall be no end."

Mary was perplexed and asked, "How shall this be, seeing I know not a man?" The angel replied, "The Holy Ghost shall come upon thee, and the power of the Highest shall overshadow thee: therefore also that holy thing which shall be born of thee shall be called the Son of God." Thus God through Gabriel offered her the vocation to be the Virgin Mother of God.

Gabriel waited. The universe and the courts of heaven were hushed. God Himself waited. Then Mary spoke, "Behold the handmaid of the Lord; be it unto me according to thy word." Of her own free will she accepted her vocation. The Word of God leapt down from heaven and by the Holy Ghost was conceived in her womb. The Incarnation took place.

The Conception of Christ was a supernatural event. It occurred in nature but was not of nature. The significance of the Incarnation lies in the fact that it was the intervention of God in the affairs of men. The human race did not and could not bring forth Christ by human generation. Christ is perfect Man, perfectly united to God. He could not have been produced by the natural process of evolution.

Natural evolution stopped with man. Man himself was evolved from lower forms of life. But then the process was brought to an abrupt halt because man by sin has refused to fulfil the purpose for which he was created, namely, to love God. He has reverted to a lower type and tries to live like an animal, seeking satisfaction in the functions of the body and in the material world. The diseased human race is not capable of producing perfect man. Left to itself, it is not evolving but degenerating, and now that we have learned to blow each other up with atom bombs, it may not have far to go before it becomes extinct. Man's specific endowments, his intellect and free will, have been turned from their appropriate end, the Vision of God, to self-seeking and conflict, with the result that man is destroying himself.

Mankind is like the motorist who, becoming lost, asked a farmer whom he met if he was on the right road to the place he was looking for. "Yes," said the farmer, "this is the right road. But you're going the wrong way." We do not want to continue in the direction in which we are traveling. We need to be turned around—to be converted. We need, not evolution, but redemption.

So Christ came and received our human nature from the Virgin Mary. Because He was conceived in her womb, He is flesh of our flesh, bone of our bone. Our blood flows in His veins. But in taking our nature He purified it, He healed it, He restored to it the qualities lost by sin. Christ is the Second Adam, the Firstborn of the redeemed race. His Conception was a new act of creation, using the stuff of the old creation, our fallen human nature, but fashioning it anew and raising it to a higher dignity than it had enjoyed before the Fall. Only God can create. Therefore, Christ was conceived in the womb of the Virgin by God the Holy Ghost.

God, however, in His tender love for man, always preserves the integrity of human personality. He wants our love. He does not want to enslave us, to make us puppets of His will. He desires our loving and, therefore, our free response. Hence, even in bestowing benefits, He respects our free will. He does not force His favors on us. He waits for us to ask, or at least to express our willingness to receive. Before He comes to us, He solicits our consent.

Had Christ incarnated Himself in a child born of two human parents, there would have been no human consent to His coming. In the act by which the child was conceived, its parents would have given consent to each other, not to God. The unborn child would have been incapable of consenting. Hence God would have had arbitrarily to destroy the person of the child in order to substitute Himself in its place. That would have been a violent and unauthorized intervention in the natural order. It would have overruled human freedom. God does not act that way.

Instead, He wooed and won the heart of the Virgin Mary. He asked her to become the Spouse of the Holy Ghost and the Mother of God Incarnate. On behalf of the human race, she gave consent. She surrendered herself to the power of the Highest. Then and then only God came to us. Perfect Lover that He is, He waited upon a maiden's will.

Mary's part in the process of our redemption is unique. She received God; she let Him become a member of the human race that He might save it from within. She welcomed Him into her womb. She carried Him, nourished His body from her own. When He was born, she held Him in her arms and fed Him from her breasts. God lay in her lap a helpless infant, dependent on her for His continued existence in this life. She sheltered Him in His tender years and provided for Him the home in which His perfect human character could develop. We, who know today how much a child's personality is shaped by his environment and how large a part his mother plays in the process, can realize how great was Mary's responsibility and why she had to be, by the fulness of the grace of God which was hers and with which she ever co-operated, the perfect Mother.

Mary's work did not end when our Lord left Nazareth to begin His public ministry. She continued to be His Mother. This meant, first of all, that she had to let Him go. It could not have been easy for her. Not only was there separation, but she undoubtedly sensed what was in store for Him. She did not hold Him back. She did not selfishly strive to make Him do her will. She wanted Him to fulfil His vocation. She, the perfect Mother, let her Child live His own life.

She claimed no special privileges from her relationship to Him. "They have no wine," she told Him at the wedding in Cana. She asked no miracle, though He performed one for her. Later we find her with His brethren when they went to investigate the rumor that He was mad. She knew it was untrue, but when she could not restrain them, she accompanied them to keep them from interfering. When our Lord refused to see them, she was not offended. He thereby had avoided the scene which she herself had been anxious to prevent. She knew He had not meant to exclude her when He said, "Whosoever shall do the will of God, the same is my brother and my sister and mother." For had she not always done the will of God?

On Calvary, she, like Him, made her supreme sacrifice of love. Without a protest, without a murmur, she gave Him to death. His enemies cried, "Come down from the cross," but not His Mother. Hers was the encouraging sympathy of silent love. His filial love responded by committing her to John's care. "Woman, behold thy son! Behold thy mother!"

We catch only these fleeting glimpses of Mary during our Lord's public ministry. They are sufficient for us to feel, as our Lord Himself felt, her presence there in the background. He could depend on her love and understanding. She, in her humility, preferred to keep out of sight. The privileges, the joy and the sorrow of her vocation as Mother of God were not things she wanted to talk about. She "kept all these things, and pondered them in her heart."

She did tell the Apostles after the Resurrection the facts of our Lord's Birth. She alone could give this information and it was important that they should have it. They needed to know that He had been conceived by the Holy Ghost in order that they might be assured that He was truly the Son of God. The Church had to be protected against thinking that the human race had produced Christ by a natural process of generation, lest we sinful human beings take credit for Him and conclude that we might achieve perfection by our own efforts. If we had already produced one perfect Man, why should we not hope that we could do so again? It is vital for us to know that the Conception of Christ was an act of God, not of man.

Mary told the story of His Birth. Of the rest, she chose to be silent. We know nothing of those wonderful hidden years of His childhood, save the account of His first visit to the Temple. We hear nothing of His visiting her during His public ministry after the first miracle in Cana; yet He was constantly in and about Nazareth and it is unthinkable that He neglected to see her. The truth is that Mary cloaked her sacred personal relationship with Christ in a mantle of silence. Hence we are not surprised that there is no record of His personal Appearances to her in His Risen Body. That she should not so much as mention them is characteristic of her.

But if Mary was not to witness to the Resurrection, what useful purpose was fulfilled by Christ's Appearances to her? The answer to that question is just the reason why we consider these Appearances important. We are prone to grade vocations by the amount of activity involved in them. Up to a point, we are right. To serve Christ in the world is indeed a tremendous privilege. To bear testimony to Him before men is a high vocation; and of all the active vocations, the Apostles' eye-witness testimony is the highest. But there is a vocation which is still higher. That is to receive Christ, to let Him enter the human race by finding a resting-place in one's heart. Such was Mary's vocation. By humble obedience, she let Christ enter her womb. She brought Him into the world and

> In her maiden bliss
> Worshipped the Beloved
> With a kiss.[2]

Now she received the Risen Christ and spent quiet hours with Him in adoring love.

Redemption is the work of God. Before we can serve Him we must know Him. Before we can show Him to others we must receive Him ourselves. To permit Him to enter the world through us is our supreme response to His love. He stands at the door of our souls and knocks. "If any man hear my voice, and open the door, I will come in to him, and will sup with him, and he with me."

We open that door a crack in our prayers, speaking to Him as it were through the doorway. We receive Him formally in our Communions, and visit with Him for a shorter or longer time—usually all too short—in the front parlor. By contemplation, however—by the surrender of ourselves to Him in adoring love, by quieting all our thoughts and feelings, by clinging to Him with a simple act of our wills—we invite Christ to stay with us. The contemplative does not treat Christ just as a visitor; rather,

[2] Christina Rosetti.

he bids Him make Himself at home. The soul who lets the Holy Spirit raise him to the highest stage of the spiritual life, the Unitive Way, goes a step further. He makes Christ the Master of his house. He knows the ultimate delight of spending all his time in rendering homage. Christ becomes the Bridegroom of the soul and they live together in sweetest intimacy.

Perhaps the Master will send forth the soul from time to time on an errand of mercy, or to minister in His name in the world or in the Church. Then the soul gladly goes as an agent of His love. But as soon as the task is accomplished, the soul hastens home to be with Christ. Perhaps the Master will permit the soul to bear some of His suffering in reparation for the sins of the world. Then the soul may exclaim with St. Paul, I "fill up that which is behind of the afflictions of Christ in my flesh for his body's sake, which is the Church." But the soul's chief contribution to the salvation of the world is that it offers Christ another dwelling-place among men, a bridgehead on which He can establish Himself and from which He can reach out to others, a tabernacle in which He may be enshrined.

Such was, above all others, the vocation of the Virgin Mary. She was the handmaid of the Lord and in her fruitful virginity she brought forth the Saviour. Such her vocation continues to be. She is still the Mother of God. As long as she abode on earth, her heart was the place where Jesus knew He was cherished and welcomed with the tenderest and purest love. Now she is Queen of Heaven, raised not only above the other saints, but above angels and archangels, above cherubim and seraphim. Her heart beats closest to the human heart of our Lord. Since through her

Christ became incarnate in the human race, so through her the human race has its most ready access to Him.

The Church has always placed the highest value on Mary's prayers. Down through the centuries the chorus of the faithful has cried, "Holy Mary, Mother of God, pray for us sinners now and in the hour of our death." We do not ask her to change her Son's mind, to alter His will. We know that she cannot and will not do that. Her will is one with His. Like Him she desires only our good. We know, however, that she, who was the Mother of Christ's human body, continues to concern herself with the welfare of the Extension of that Body, the Church. If we are honestly humble, we recognize that we need her help in lifting up our feeble prayers to Christ. We want her to ask for us what we in our blindness do not know we need. We beg her to take us by the hand and lead us to her Son. As one of the traditional prayers of the Church puts it, we say to her through whom Christ first came to us in this world, "Hereafter, when our earthly exile shall be ended, show us Jesus, the blessed Fruit of thy womb."

XII

Rule and Governance

After that, he was seen of James.

I CORINTHIANS 15:7

When St. Paul speaks of James he always means the first Bishop of Jerusalem. This man occupied so prominent a place in the early Christian community that his name was enough to designate him. Yet there are few Gospel characters about whom we have as little information as about James the Less. Without any warning or explanation we suddenly discover, in the Book of Acts, that he is head of the Mother Church at Jerusalem.

He is called "the Lord's brother." This cannot mean he was a full brother to our Lord, since our Lord had no human father. It cannot mean that he was a half-brother to our Lord, for the Virgin Mary had but one Child. The Church has always been certain of this. It has found it unbelievable that she, whose consecrated virginity was sanctified and made fruitful by the Holy Ghost, should subsequently have surrendered that virginity to a human husband. She who was called to the supreme vocation of Mother of God would not have become the mother of other children. "This gate shall be shut, it shall not be opened, and no man shall enter in by it; because the Lord, the God of Israel, hath entered in by it, therefore it shall be shut."

The various references in the New Testament to the "brethren of the Lord" are not refutations of the Church's tradition. For the word "brethren" is ambiguous. With us, its meaning has become limited so that it designates only the children of the same parents. But more primitive people, among whom tribal or family feeling is strong, employ the term to cover relationships at least as remote as cousins. Even today, we find the native Africans using the word in this sense. It was common practice among the Jews of our Lord's time. Hence, we may assume that His brethren stood in some kind of family relationship to Him; but we are not justified in asserting that they were His brothers in our modern restricted meaning of the word. He was His Mother's only Child.

Some object to believing in Mary's continued virginity on the grounds that it implies a slur against marriage and the begetting of children. It is thought to mean that sex is considered to be tainted with evil and that, therefore, in order to maintain her purity, Mary would have nothing to do with it. This interpretation of the Church's teaching is entirely false. Our Lord was born of a Virgin not because this was a purer method of conception, but because it permitted mankind, in the person of Mary, to give, or had she so chosen, to withhold, consent to the Incarnation. God did not force Himself on the human race. He wooed and won a maiden's love. Mary remained a virgin because, having given herself, body and soul, to God, there was no room left for a similar self-bestowal to a human husband. Joseph neither asked nor expected it of her. He recognized from the first that his rôle was that of protector and provider for the infant God-made-Man.

The same Church which insists that Mary remained a virgin also asserts that marriage can and should be Holy Matrimony. It provides a sacrament by which a man and woman are ushered into the closest and most sacred of human relationships. They are to give themselves to each other without reservation for life. The working out and making good of the marriage vow is the school of love which prepares the man and woman for heaven, for loving union with God. On the physical level, sex is the channel of their mutual self-oblation. When it is used for this purpose, it fulfils the holy function for which it was bestowed upon mankind.

The establishment of this ideal of Christian marriage, however, depends directly on the reverence in which the Church has held the Mother of God, both for her part in the Incarnation and for her consecrated virginity. The former was the lever which raised woman from a position in which she was equated—as in the Tenth Commandment—with a man's house, his servant, his maid, his ox, and his ass. The fact that it was a woman, not a man, who, on behalf of the human race, gave consent and bore the responsibility of the Incarnation, forced men to recognize women as human beings of equal dignity with themselves. The Church's gratitude to Mary and its desire for her prayers encouraged the further exaltation of womanhood. This attitude is essential to the possibility of Christian marriage. It is only when a man respects his wife as a person with equal rights and privileges that a truly loving union can be formed between them.

Mary's continuance in her state of consecrated virginity has been the inspiration to men and women of every generation to dedicate themselves to Christ in the same state. This is also necessary to the upholding of the ideal of Holy Matrimony. For a life-long marital faithfulness demands control and restraint of the sex urge by both parties to the marriage. There is marital chastity as well as celibate chastity. In this age, when we suffer from a phobia on the subject of sex, when some psychiatrists seem to imply that health demands an unrestrained indulgence of the sex appetite, we need testimony to the fact that, by the grace of God, the sex urge can be controlled. The most impressive form of that testimony is to be found in those whom God calls to give themselves to Him directly in this life, to forego marriage and to control the sex impulse completely by not using it at all. Those whom God calls to celibacy, who are faithful in using the grace God provides, are able to maintain this complete restraint and do not become warped, frustrated old maids and bachelors—as anyone who knows them can testify. They are a living refutation of the assertion that chastity is either impossible or unhealthy.

We cannot be certain just what James' relationship to our Lord was. Some have suggested that James was a son of Joseph by a previous marriage. This is a plausible guess, but it conflicts with the tradition that James is to be identified with the son of Alphaeus, mentioned as one of the Twelve. All of the New Testament references which have been taken as indicating James' parentage can be reconciled. The result is a bit complicated; but family relationships often are.

It is customary to assume that James' father was Alphaeus and his mother "the other Mary." This Mary is described as the mother of James the Less and Joses by the first two Gospels, and they list both James and Joses among the brethren of the Lord. Now, if Alphaeus was the brother[1] of the Virgin Mary, this would bring things out right. For Mary, whom we take to be his wife, is described by St. John as the Virgin's sister. It is highly improbable that two daughters in the same family should both be named Mary. But the two Marys could easily have been sisters-in-law.

If Alphaeus died while his children were young, that would account for his wife's taking them to live with the Holy Family in Nazareth. That they all lived together there would seem to be the strong implication of the first two Gospels. The residents of Nazareth are the ones who associate Jesus with His brethren. Of Him they asked, "Is not this the Carpenter, the Son of Mary, the Brother of James, and Joses, and of Juda, and Simon? and are not His sisters here with us?" Clearly, they all lived in the same town, if not in the same house. At some later date, apparently, Mary, the mother of our Lord's brethren, married Cleophas, as whose wife she is described by St. John.

Supposing that all this is true, we still know very little about James. Apart from the lists of the Twelve, he is never mentioned during the Lord's ministry. He does not seem to have had any exceptional talents nor to have sought a position of prominence. He was content to be one of the

---

[1] Some might prefer to make him a half-brother, son of either Joachim or Anne by a former marriage, in order to preserve the tradition that Mary was the only child of their marriage to each other.

unnoticed figures in the background until our Lord called him to a greater responsibility. The Book of Acts makes it clear that James was equal to the task that was given him. He was an excellent leader of the early Church. But his previous obscurity indicates that the choice of him for the Bishopric of Jerusalem owed much to the inspiration of the Holy Ghost. This should always be true in the selection of authorities in the Church.

Our Lord's Appearance to James undoubtedly was to prepare him for the authority and responsibility which ultimately were to be his. It was not, however, the means by which he was appointed Bishop of Jerusalem. For some time after the Ascension, Peter was head of the local Church and John seems to have been his lieutenant. The first time James appears in a position of prominence is in Galatians 1:19, when Paul, after his conversion, visited the Apostles; but even there he seems to be in second place to Peter. In Acts, he is first mentioned in 12:17, where again he seems to be second in command. Perhaps he became in the full sense head of the Jerusalem Church at that time when Peter, after his release from prison by an angel, "departed and went into another place." Had James been appointed Bishop of Jerusalem by the Risen Christ, there would not have been this delay in his taking office. But his appointment did not rest on a private revelation, on his own claim to have been called. Those whom Christ calls to public office He appoints through public channels. Thus their authority is objectively accredited.

We have not the slightest hint of what occurred during the Risen Christ's Appearance to James. Presumably the latter was not told specifically what was in store for him;

nor was he given directions as to how he should act or what decisions he should make as Bishop of Jerusalem. That is not our Lord's way of guiding us. He gives us the inspiration we need at the time we need it. "Take no thought how or what ye shall speak: for it shall be given you in that same hour what ye shall speak." It is more likely that Christ appeared to James in order to stimulate in him a deep humility, an utter dependence on God, a constancy in righteousness and prayer. If so, James learned his lesson well. Tradition tells us he was conspicuous for his humble devotion. Because he had developed by God's grace this type of character, he was a fit person to rule the Jerusalem Church and to preside at the Council of the Apostles.

There are two kinds of authority which are conferred on the officials of the Church. First, there is the authority to teach and to act as ministers of Christ. In the next chapter we shall watch our Lord bestowing that power on all the Apostles and we shall consider there its purpose and implications. Second, there is the authority to rule and govern. It is for the reception of that authority that James was prepared in this Appearance.

Christ was not, in the strict sense of the word, a lawgiver. He laid down certain fundamental principles of faith and practice. He left it to the Church, under the guidance of the Holy Spirit, to formulate those principles into specific laws. The Church has done so. The law of Faith has been laid down in the Creeds, in the decisions of General Councils. The law of practice has been crystallized in the precepts of the Church and in the canons and various other enactments which it has been inspired to make from time to time.

But this general law still needs to be interpreted and applied to changing local situations and to the circumstances of individual lives. We need to know how and when the law is to be kept under the conditions in which we find ourselves at the moment. This is tremendously important. We can do God's will only if we know what He requires of us. God has not left us to our own devices, to our own feeble insights, in answering this question. He has placed the responsibility for making these decisions and interpretations in the hands of such officials of the Church as James was to be in Jerusalem. Through them, we can find out just what is our bounden duty in regard to worship, prayer, penitence, self-discipline, alms-giving, and service.

Another way in which God's authority is mediated to men is through the officers of the State. As St. Paul tells us, "There is no power but of God: the powers that be are ordained of God." God wants human society to be regulated in justice, prudence, and peace. His moral law is to be applied to secular affairs. To this end, He gives His authority to the legitimately chosen officials of the State. In the course of history, there have been many forms of government, each with its own method of choosing its rulers. But no matter how they may be chosen, God is the source of their authority and they are responsible to Him.

Democracy has suffered as a form of government because it has not recognized this truth. Its enemies have described it as mob-rule (which is the literal translation of its etymological roots). If we consider that its elected officials derive their authority from the voters and are responsible to them, then democracy is in fact mob-rule and its leaders will normally be demagogs—people who can appeal to the crowd. Self-perpetuation in office becomes the test of the successful exercise of authority, and, therefore, the first object must be to use authority in such a way as will please the people and win votes. Moral considerations, justice, honesty, and farsightedness will be secondary to expediency as determinants of public policy.

This difficulty is not, however, inherent in democracy itself. It is a form of government compatible with the recognition of the divine origin of authority. Its officials are designated by popular vote, but the determining factor in casting one's vote should be the fitness of the candidate to exercise the authority which his office confers upon him; and the latter should realize that he must answer before the bar of divine judgment for his exercise of that authority. This recognition of the divine origin of secular authority and of the sacred responsibility in exercising it will make the leaders of a democracy statesmen instead of politicians. Nothing else can. The key to a sound democracy is a clear understanding of the limitation of the rôle of the people. Under such a government, the people have the right to choose their rulers. They do not have the right to rule their rulers. To claim the latter would be to defeat the purpose of authority, which is to enable rulers to rule.

In this age of rampant individualism, the thought of a ruler's ruling is abhorrent to many. We are told that State officials are not rulers at all. They are servants of the people. We do not dispute that their function is to serve the people. But how do they best serve them? By letting the people determine policy on the basis of selfish interest and short-term expediency? Hardly. The official who truly serves is the one who uses his authority to direct the people—in spite of their mistaken wishes, if necessary—toward the best and wisest course. In a word, officials in a democracy —as in every other kind of government—serve the people best by ruling them. This is what they are elected to do. They should use the power placed in their hands for the people's good, not for the people's pleasure. As long and as far as they recognize their responsibility to God in the exercise of their authority, there will be no danger of tyranny. If they do not recognize that responsibility, they should not be elected in the first place.

We must not limit the concept of ruler to the chiefs of Church and State. Popes and primates, archbishops and bishops are endowed with Christ's spiritual authority; but so, also, are priests and pastors in their lesser spheres. Likewise, in the State, emperors and kings, presidents and governors share the exercise of secular authority with judges and legislators, with the sheriff in his county and with the cop on his beat. They are all representatives of the law which is ultimately God's law. Nor is rule and governance to be found only in Church and State. There are other areas of life in which men have a limited but real authority over their fellows: the employer over his employees, the foreman over his crew, the labor leader over the members of his union, the teacher over his pupils, the conductor over his orchestra, the captain over his team, the president of a club over its members. All have, to some degree, the responsibility of making decisions for others and of giving directions to them. Finally, in the most basic social unit of all, there is the rule of a father over his family and of both parents over the children.

It is not only in order to achieve order and efficiency

that God has delegated His authority to men. The provision that, in all departments of human society, some shall
command and others shall carry out their orders has for its
purpose the training of us in love. Both in submission to
authority and in the exercise of it we are given the opportunity to obey. Obedience, in Christian thought, is an
activity of positive value. St. Augustine calls it the mother
of all virtues. We can readily see why this is so. Pride is the
root of all sin; its opposite, humility, must be the root of
all virtue. Obedience is simply humility in action. It is
surrendering oneself to God as He expresses Himself clearly
and definitely through duly constituted authority. "Thy
will, not mine, be done."

Man is created to depend, to hang on God. He is a vine,
not a tree; he cannot stand upright without support. God
has ordained the powers that be to serve as a trellis on
which the vine of the soul may climb and expand. Thus
authority is not designed to repress or enslave man, but to
liberate him. The modern tendency to minimize law and to
eliminate authority rips down the soul and tramples it in
the muck of selfishness. To prevent this, God wills that His
authority, mediated through men, shall be enforced. He
expects rulers and governors to bear not the sword in vain.
(Church authorities should restrict themselves, of course,
to the "sword of the spirit," imposing only spiritual, not
material and physical, penalties.) Enforced authority is
better than down-trodden vines. Obedience bears its full
fruit, however, only when it is willing and prompt. Then
it becomes an expression of love. Pride makes us want to
have our own way. Love means "carrying out another's
wishes as though they were our own."

But can we trust human authorities always to command aright? They are fallible as we are. Will they not make mistakes? Will they not often be impelled by selfish motives? They will. But unless their commands are manifestly sinful, it is better to obey than to indulge in headstrong opposition, at least until such time as they can be deprived of office by due process of law. The surrender of our self-will is more important in God's eyes than mere efficiency. He would rather see us do something less good in itself because we are told to do it than to seek a higher good in defiance of authority. He will not let us lose our way because we are misdirected. Submission to authority is itself the highest way. It is our opportunity to take the lowest place, to surrender, in the last analysis, to God Himself, to grow in humble love.

Not many of us, however, no matter how shy and retiring we may be, are likely to get through life without having, sooner or later, to exercise authority. We may escape great prominence and responsibility. But in one capacity or another, God calls most men to take command of others. This is an occasion for a still higher form of obedience. For the authority which is given to us, however small in scale and narrow in scope, is God's authority. In exercising it we must at all times conform to His will. Here, as in all else, Christ is the Model. He said, "I came down from heaven, not to do mine own will, but the will of him that sent me." Hence, those to whom Christ commits the governance of others should strive to imitate Him. Christ would not bind on men burdens too heavy to be borne, for His yoke is easy and His burden light. On the other hand, He did not water down God's law to make it palatable to popular taste. He did not withhold rebuke and censure when it was deserved. Nevertheless, a bruised reed He would not break and a dimly-burning flax He would not quench. He always sought to encourage the best in those to whom He ministered. Above all, He led rather than drove men to God. "Learn of me; for I am meek and lowly in heart." Christ expects the same of those who rule in His name.

To have, even in the slightest degree and for a brief period, command over one's fellows is a grave responsibility and one for which we shall have to render a strict account. It is terrifyingly easy to misuse authority for selfish gain or for self-aggrandizement. The result is unfaithfulness to God, injury to others, and loss of one's own soul. No one who realizes this would presumptuously seek or grasp power. Yet if one is called to exercise it, one must not hold back. We do not govern in our own strength. We can count on God's guidance and help. In this Appearance to James, Christ prepared him for the exercise of the authority which was to be conferred upon him. He will likewise equip us through the means of grace which He gives us, when we are called to rule and governance. If we perform its duties with selfless humility, we shall receive the gracious commendation, "Well done, good and faithful servant; thou hast been faithful over a few things, I will make thee ruler over many things: enter thou into the joy of thy Lord."

XIII

Apostolate

Then of all the apostles.

I CORINTHIANS 15:7.

Then the eleven disciples went away into Galilee, into a mountain where Jesus had appointed them. And when they saw him, they worshipped him: but some doubted. And Jesus came and spake unto them, saying, All power is given unto me in heaven and in earth. Go yet therefore, and teach all nations, baptizing them in the name of the Father, and of the Son, and of the Holy Ghost: teaching them to observe all things whatsoever I have commanded you: and, lo, I am with you alway, even unto the end of the world.

ST. MATTHEW 28:16-20.

And he said unto them, Go ye into all the world, and preach the gospel to every creature. He that believeth and is baptized shall be saved; but he that believeth not shall be damned. And these signs shall follow them that believe; In my name shall they cast out devils; they shall speak with new tongues; they shall take up serpents; and if they drink any deadly thing, it shall not hurt them; they shall lay hands on the sick, and they shall recover.

ST. MARK 16:15-18.

Then said Jesus to them again, Peace be unto you: as my Father hath sent me, even so send I you. And when he had said this, he breathed on them, and saith unto them, Receive ye the Holy Ghost: whose soever sins ye remit, they are re-mitted unto them; and whose soever sins ye retain, they are retained.

ST. JOHN 20:21-23.

We come now to another Appearance in Galilee, this time to the disciples who were to be the first official ministers of the Church. These were the Twelve to whose training our Lord had devoted so much time and effort during His public ministry. But one of them, Judas, had fallen from the high vocation to which he was called and, in despair, had hanged himself. So there were only eleven left to meet on "a mountain where Jesus had appointed them." To them the Risen Christ appeared. "And when they saw him, they worshipped him."

Our Lord began by reminding them that all power was given unto Him in heaven and in earth. He is King of kings and Lord of lords. He is "God of God, Light of Light, Very God of Very God." He was the Father's Agent in creation, "by whom all things were made." "All things were created by him, and for him. And he is before all things, and by him all things consist." He is the Revelation of the Father, "the Image of the invisible God." As He said to Philip, "He that hath seen me hath seen the Father." He is God translated into human terms. He was sent by the Father into the world "that the world through him might be saved." In Him "we have redemption through his blood, even the forgiveness of sins." He has "delivered us from the power of darkness" and translated us into His Kingdom. "He is the Head of the Body, the Church: who is the Beginning, the Firstborn from the dead." "For it pleased the Father that in him should all fulness dwell; and, having made peace through the blood of his cross, by him to reconcile all things unto himself."

Now to His disciples He said, "As my Father hath sent me, even so send I you." As He was the Agent of the

Father in bringing revelation, redemption, and new life
to them, so they were to be His agents through whom the
work of God Incarnate would be continued on earth. This
Appearance ended with a promise, "Lo, I am with you
alway, even unto the end of the world." Its purpose was
to instruct and commission the Apostles as the means
through which that promise was to be kept.

We have now reached the heart of the Christian dispensation. It alone among all religions makes the claim
that God Himself, the one God, the only God, the Creator
of heaven and earth, became Man. He did not just appear
to be man. He really took a human nature and lived a
human life. He was born as a Baby. He grew up. He worked
as a Carpenter. He taught men by word and example what
God is like. Finally, He was arrested, condemned, crucified,
and put to death. Still this did not terminate the Incarnation. He rose from the dead. He ascended into heaven. God
the Son never ceased being God, of course. But now He
reigns in heaven as both God and Man.

But has God ceased to be incarnate here on earth? If
that were so, the world would have suffered a grievous
loss. Those who lived in Galilee and Jerusalem during the
few years when Jesus walked among men would have had
a tremendous advantage over the rest of us. They could
know God as a personal Friend. They could talk with
Him, eat with Him, live with Him. His teaching was expounded in their own language, in words which they could
hear with their ears. They could bring their troubles to
Him and He could answer their questions, heal their bodies, forgive their sins. To His disciples He was, as St.
John tells us, "That . . . which we have heard, which we

have seen with our eyes, which we have looked upon, and our hands have handled, of the Word of life."

Is all that ended now? Is the Incarnation, as far as its manifestation in this world is concerned, simply a historical fact that happened long ago, something we learn about but cannot now experience? Are we left with second-hand accounts of what God once did, and with a purely spiritual relationship with Him? Has Christ provided no means by which He can continue to speak to us, no means by which He can reach out to us, using the material world as the channel of communication? We need that objective contact with Him as much as the original disciples did. In this life, experiences which come to us through the senses carry a conviction and assurance that no subjective spiritual experience can ever have. The latter may always be a matter of self-deception. It contains a large emotional ingredient, and, if we know anything about ourselves, we know that our emotions are not reliable. They provide an unstable basis for our relationship with God. On the other hand, experiences which are embodied in the material world have an objective validity. They persist independently of our moods. They are hard facts. Does Christ still come to us on this level of dependable experience?

He does. The Incarnation persists as a practical reality on earth. When our Lord ascended in His Risen and Glorified Body to heaven, He made for Himself another form of that same Body through which He can continue to speak and act on earth. That new form of His Body is the Church. It is not made up of cells of flesh and blood; it is composed of the souls and bodies of baptized Christians.

This enables it to outlast the centuries and to encircle the globe. Nevertheless, though its form has changed, it is an Extension of the same Body, and through it He can express Himself just as definitely and objectively on the material and social level of our experience as He did in Galilee and Jerusalem. We do not have to sigh with nostalgic sentimentality,

> I think when I read that sweet story of old,
> When Jesus was here among men,
> How He called little children as lambs to His Fold:
> I should like to have been with them then.

The Man Christ Jesus is with us today in His Body the Church. The Church is the Extension of the Incarnation.

The first members—that is, organic parts—of Christ's Body the Church were those eleven disciples whom He met on a mountain in Galilee. They were to receive their full incorporation into Christ on the ensuing Feast of Pentecost, as we shall see in the next chapter. But the eleven were also to have certain special functions and responsibilities in the Body not shared by all the other members. They were to be Apostles. In the Appearance we are now considering, the Risen Christ explained their duties and conferred the Apostolate upon them.

St. Matthew's account indicates the two chief aspects of their office. First, they were to preach the Gospel. "Go ye therefore, and teach all nations, . . . teaching them to observe all things whatsoever I have commanded you." Already He had committed to them His message, in words so compelling that they had burned themselves into the memories of the disciples. For three years, in those same Galilean hills where now they communed with Him, He had taught them in terse and pithy epigrams, in parables and allegories drawn from the events of common life, in poems such as the Beatitudes. They had watched Him as He went about doing good. They had seen His character expressed in His dealings with the men and women who came to Him for help. Finally, they had been with Him during those terrible last days in Jerusalem when He had met and conquered His enemies by love, when He had laid down His life for the sheep. Now they beheld Him risen from the dead in triumphant glory. They knew the Gospel by heart.

It takes more than knowledge to teach. One must also have authority. This, Christ now conferred upon them. They were commissioned to speak in Christ's name. In a few days, this authority would be confirmed by the gift of the Holy Spirit, who would guide them into all truth. Under His inspiration they would be able to preach and to interpret the Gospel. They would commit it to writing. They and their successors would draw out its implications and express them in theological language. These would be summarized into Creeds, formulated in the decisions of General Councils. In all this, they would not be expressing their own opinions, their own philosophy. They would be acting as the mouthpiece of Christ, who is the Word of God. God Himself would be speaking through them.

They were witnesses to, not creators of, the Gospel. The Christian Faith was delivered to them. They transmitted it to others. The authority resided in the Faith, not in them as individuals. We do not believe the Apostles because we consider them to have been brilliant thinkers who were able to discover the truth about God and man. We believe them because we know that they were trustworthy witnesses to a revelation received from God which He commanded and empowered them to hand on to others. Down through the centuries, that unchanging Faith has passed from generation to generation, "Jesus Christ the same yesterday, and today, and forever."

Therefore, the Christian teacher is under the most solemn obligation to teach the Faith, the whole Faith, and nothing but the Faith. He must preserve the integrity of the Gospel. He should not, on the one hand, limit his teaching to those doctrines that appeal to him as reasonable and important. If he does, he will defeat the purpose of the Faith, which is to expand our knowledge and to correct the bias of contemporary thought. *Credo ut intelligam.* "I believe in order that I may know." Those who teach only popular doctrines will be omitting those elements in the Faith which people most need to hear. On the other hand, the official teacher should be careful to add nothing to the Gospel. He must not elevate his own opinions to the status of revealed truth. Like St. Paul, he must be able to say, "I have kept the faith . . . I delivered unto you. . . . that which I also received." When a minister of the Word fulfils his vocation to be the guardian and transmitter of the sacred tradition, our Lord is able through him to teach us as clearly and directly as He did the multitudes who heard His words beside the Galilean Lake or in the Temple courts.

But Christ wants to do more than speak to us. He wants to reach out to us as well, taking the material things of this world and expressing Himself through them to strengthen and assist us. The acts of Christ in His Body the Church are called "sacraments." He has designed them to meet our spiritual needs, and since they take the form of an outward and visible action, they have that quality of objective assurance which inheres in experiences that come to us by way of our bodily senses.

The sacraments are covenants which Christ has made with us. He has promised that when certain simple, external rites are performed by the members of His Church, He will convey certain spiritual benefits on the souls of those who participate in them. Of course, the sacraments are not magic. God does His part if the requirements He has laid down are met. But the recipient must willingly and reverently accept the benefits offered. He must by faith recognize and lay hold on the grace which God bestows. He must use the grace in his daily living. Otherwise, the sacraments will have no effect on his soul. Worse than that, if he receives the sacraments irreverently, if he spurns the love which God seeks to convey to him, if he neglects to use the grace received, he is committing sacrilege and burdening his soul with yet another sin. Just because God does His part when a sacrament is validly administered, it is God Himself whom we insult and reject when we misuse it.

The objective assurance of the sacraments, however, depends on their outward and visible actions being performed exactly as Christ directed. He set the terms to which His promises are attached. We cannot be sure of obtaining the promise on any other grounds. It is for this reason, not for any love of legalistic detail, that the Church has defined for us with great care and accuracy what the external requirements of the sacraments are. When they have been carried out, we know that God makes the corresponding grace available because He has promised it.

St. Matthew's account of the Appearance to the eleven tells us that the Risen Christ bade them "teach all nations, baptizing them in the Name of the Father, and of the Son, and of the Holy Ghost." This is the first sacrament which a soul receives. Baptism lays the foundations of the Christian life. By it, the soul is cleansed from the taint of original sin and is absolved from any actual sins which he may have committed. He is incorporated into Christ and made henceforth a member of His Body. God the Holy Spirit takes up His abode in the baptized soul, bringing with Him the virtues of faith, hope, and love, and His manifold gifts.

The symbolic act of washing is appropriate to the purifying aspects of this sacrament. The dedication of the person in the Name of the Trinity shows that he is devoted to God, as He revealed Himself in Christ, and is thenceforth possessed by Him. The baptized person receives at this time his Christian name, indicating that he has been reborn as a child of God.

God wants the soul to have the grace of Baptism at the earliest possible moment. Those who object to infant Baptism have failed to understand its true nature. They think of it as the act by which we "join the Church." Therefore, they argue, it must be a deliberate, conscious choice on our part. Now, it is true that we are made members of the Church by Baptism. This is effected, however, not by what we do, but by what God does. We do not join the Church, make ourselves members. No amount of deciding or wanting to belong to the Church will, of itself, incorporate us. Food cannot incorporate itself into a body. The body assimilates the food. So Christ, through His Body the Church, assimilates us into Himself.

Consent is, as always, necessary. But in the case of infants, consent is given in their names by their sponsors. The sponsors thereby incur the solemn responsibility (whence the name) to assure that the child, as he grows older, understands the benefits which he has received and the obligations to which he has been committed.

St. John mentions the directions for another sacrament which the Risen Christ gave to His disciples. "Whose soever sins ye remit, they are remitted unto them; and whose soever sins ye retain, they are retained." Be it noted that they were authorized not only to forgive sins but also to refuse to forgive them. There is only one ground for such a refusal; namely, that the person asking forgiveness is not penitent. Hence, in order to exercise this function, the minister must have the opportunity to judge the petitioner's penitence. Anyone who wishes to receive sacramental forgiveness must confess his sins and demonstrate his penitence in the minister's presence. The early Church required this to take the form of public confession in the presence of the bishop and the whole congregation. As that led to scandal and other grave abuses, the Church was guided by the Holy Spirit to substitute private confession to a priest under the seal of the confessional.

The purpose of the sacrament of Absolution is to deal with post-baptismal sin. Unfortunately, Christians do sin after Baptism and that sacrament cannot be repeated. A definite and objective way of disposing of the accumulation of sin from time to time and of renewing grace in the

soul is therefore needed. Our Lord has, of course, anticipated this need and provided for it. After finding out our
sins by careful self-examination, we can have the experience of apologizing for them in the presence of another
human being. In return, Christ assures us, through the
words of the priest which we can hear with our ears, that
we are forgiven. At the same time, since every sacrament
has its positive as well as its negative side, we receive the
spiritual grace we require to cope successfully with our
particular temptations.

Still another sacrament is mentioned in the summary of
the Resurrection Appearances at the end of St. Mark's
Gospel. "They shall lay hands on the sick, and they shall
recover." St. James, in his Epistle, is more specific. "Is
any sick among you? let him call for the elders of the
Church; and let them pray over him, anointing him with
oil in the name of the Lord: and the prayer of faith shall
save the sick, and the Lord shall raise him up; and if he
have committed sins, they shall be forgiven him." Thus
Christ continues His ministry of healing through His Body
the Church in the sacrament called "Holy Unction." Of
course, the Church does not guarantee miraculously to heal
all who are sick; though our Lord often uses Unction for
that purpose. When, however, the person is called to bear
a long illness, the sacrament conveys the grace to accept it
patiently and to endure it profitably. If the time has come
for the soul to depart this life, Unction prepares him for
the great experience of death.

The greatest of all the sacraments, the one in which the
Risen Christ most obviously fulfils His promise to be with
us till the end of time, is the Eucharist, or Holy Com-

munion. Our Lord demonstrated the outward and visible sign of this sacrament when He instituted it at the Last Supper. He took bread and wine and said over them, "This is my body . . . This is my blood." Thereupon He commanded His Apostles, "This do in remembrance of me."

The implications of the Eucharist are too vast and its benefits too numerous to be more than touched on here. Christ makes Himself really present, both as God and as Man, under the forms of bread and wine. The same love which went up from His human heart on the cross is in His heart on the altar. He puts Himself into our hands that we may re-present His perfect love to the Father as our own act of worship. When we receive Communion, He enters our souls to feed and strengthen us with Himself.

Our Lord's issuance of His directions for administering the three remaining sacraments is not recorded for us. It is not difficult to explain this omission. In Holy Matrimony, the outward action is simply the vow of life-long fidelity made to each other by the bride and groom. This did not represent any important change over the current Jewish customs. But for baptized persons, it is a true sacrament through which is bestowed the grace for mutual self-giving and for the establishment of a Christian home.

Likewise, in Confirmation and Holy Orders, the rite was already familiar to the Apostles. The laying on of hands was the traditional Jewish manner of giving a solemn blessing or of commissioning a man for a special work. The Evangelists, therefore, did not consider it necessary to record our Lord's instructions to use this ceremony, together with the invocation of the Holy Spirit, as the means whereby the soul's capacity for the gifts of the

Spirit is increased in Confirmation, and the grace of Holy Orders is bestowed in Ordination. Shortly after Pentecost, we find the Apostles administering these sacraments and giving every indication that, in so doing, they were acting in accordance with Christ's commands.

Besides knowing how to perform the sacramental rites, the Apostles had also to be given the authority and power to administer them. For the sacraments are acts of Christ. In order to express Himself outwardly and visibly in this present world, He uses a human agent. But the acts of that agent are valid only if he has been authorized by Christ.

A legal analogy will help us here.[1] If John Doe on his own authority draws checks on Richard Roe's bank account or signs contracts in his name, John Doe commits a crime. But if Richard Roe gives John Doe a power of attorney authorizing him to do these things, then John Doe is acting legally and his signature binds Richard Roe. They are, in fact, Richard Roe's acts. The power of attorney, however, must be a document duly signed and sealed. It is not enough for John Doe to believe himself called to act as Richard Roe's agent, or to think that he has been told to do so. He must have objective proof that will stand up in a court of law, in the event that any of the transactions are questioned. And if he is to be authorized to commission other agents to act in Richard Roe's name, that also must be included in the powers originally granted.

In like manner, the Risen Christ specifically commissioned the Apostles to act in His name. Their official acts were to be His acts. When they performed the external requirements of a sacrament, our Lord bound Himself to

[1] See "Power of Attorney," in *The Holy Cross Magazine*, September, 1944.

bestow the appropriate grace. Only thus are sacraments possible. The Apostles could not, in their own strength, produce the effects promised in the sacraments. No man is skilful enough or holy enough to forgive sin or to command Christ to be present under the forms of bread and wine. God alone can do these things. But because He wants to do them through men, He authorized and empowered the Apostles to be His agents.

The Apostles, in turn, passed this commission on to their successors through the Sacrament of Holy Orders. To some men they gave but a part of their Apostolic function. Deacons may only assist the higher clergy in certain restricted ways. Priests are empowered to administer all the sacraments except Confirmation and Holy Orders. That is, they are not authorized to commission other agents. To the bishops, on the other hand, was given the fulness of the sacramental power and authority which the Apostles had received from Christ.

Holy Orders, then, is the spiritual "power of attorney" to act in Christ's name. Our Lord bestowed it upon the Apostles. They conferred it on the first bishops by a definite, objective action, the laying on of hands. It has come down from generation to generation in an unbroken tactual succession to the bishops of the contemporary Church. They and the lower clergy whom they ordain are able to administer the sacraments on the basis of the same commission the Apostles received from Christ. Just as their authority as ministers of the Word resides in the Faith which they transmit and not in their own ideas and insights, so their authority as ministers of the sacraments resides in their Ordination, not in their moral character.

Whether they are good men or bad, their official acts are valid. This makes it all the more imperative that the minister maintain a moral character appropriate to his sacred office. Otherwise, he is a source of scandal to Christ in His Church. But although few men, in spite of their best efforts, succeed in attaining to anything like the holiness of Christ, our Lord is willing to use sinners as His ministers in order that He may continue to manifest Himself objectively in this world. When they teach the Faith, He speaks through their lips. When they, having been duly ordained, administer the sacraments, He conveys through them the promised grace. Thus Christ reaches out from first century Palestine right down to our own time and place.

"I am the vine, ye are the branches." The Vine has borne much fruit. Throughout the centuries it has grown, putting out its runners in all directions. Today, it is a vast and complicated network of branches reaching even into the darkest corners of the globe. Human sin has, alas, to some extent ravished the Vine. It has broken off some of the branches. It has blighted others, decreasing their fruitfulness. In some places, the Vine has been entangled in itself so that the branches grate against each other, crowd each other out. Perhaps the day is not far off when the Husbandman will prune the Vine, cutting out the dead wood, reengrafting the severed branches, purging the others that they may bring forth more fruit. But in spite of its present outward appearance of confusion and even, at times, of barrenness, it is still, in so far as it is alive at all, the one true Vine, the roots of which are in that mountain in Galilee where the Risen Lord bestowed the Apostolate on His first disciples.

XIV

He Was Taken Up

And, behold, I send the promise of my Father upon you: but tarry ye in the city of Jerusalem, until ye be endued with power from on high. And he led them out as far as to Bethany, and he lifted up his hands, and blessed them. And it came to pass, while he blessed them, he was parted from them, and carried up into heaven. And they worshipped him, and returned to Jerusalem with great joy: and were continually in the temple, praising and blessing God.

ST. LUKE 24:49-53.

The former treatise have I made, O Theophilus, of all that Jesus began both to do and teach, until the day in which he was taken up, after that he through the Holy Ghost had given commandments unto the Apostles whom he had chosen: to whom also he shewed himself alive after his passion by many infallible proofs, being seen of them forty days, and speaking of the things pertaining to the kingdom of God: and, being assembled together with them, commanded them that they should not depart from Jerusalem, but wait for the promise of the Father, which, saith he, ye have heard of me. For John truly baptized with water; but ye shall be baptized with the Holy Ghost not many days hence. When they therefore were come together, they asked of him, saying, Lord, wilt thou at this time restore again the kingdom to Israel? And he said unto them, It is not for you to know the times or the seasons, which the Father hath put in his own power. But ye shall receive power, after that the Holy Ghost is come upon you: and ye shall be witnesses unto me both in Jerusalem, and in all Judaea, and in Samaria, and unto the uttermost part of the earth. And when

*he had spoken these things, while they beheld, he was taken up;
and a cloud received him out of their sight. And while they
looked stedfastly toward heaven as he went up, behold, two
men stood by them in white apparel; which also said, Ye men
of Galilee, why stand ye gazing up into heaven? this same Jesus,
which is taken up from you into heaven, shall so come in like
manner as ye have seen him go into heaven. Then returned they
unto Jerusalem from the mount called Olivet, which is from
Jerusalem a sabbath day's journey.*

ACTS I:I-I2

St. Luke gives us two accounts of our Lord's final Appearance to His disciples, one in his Gospel and the other in
Acts. In the first, the Ascension might seem to follow immediately after the Appearance of Christ on Easter night.
This, of course, is impossible. It would not leave time for
the other recorded Appearances and St. Luke precludes this
false impression by saying in Acts that our Lord was "seen
of them forty days." But the fact that his Gospel runs the
two events together makes it probable that the latter
started where the former had occurred, in the Upper
Room.

It was most appropriate that our Lord's final Appearance
should take place in the Holy City. There He had entered
into His Kingdom on Palm Sunday. There He had won His
Kingdom on Good Friday. Now He was about to establish
that Kingdom among men. It was not a new kingdom, but
was the continuation and the sublimation of the old. It
fulfilled the purpose for which the Jews were the Chosen
People. Many of them, especially the official leaders, refused
to follow Christ from the old Israel into the new. Our

Lord had had to train and authorize new leaders to take their places. But the continuity was emphasized by having the new dispensation emanate from the capital of the old. Therefore, He assembled His disciples in Jerusalem to terminate His Resurrection Appearances and to prepare them to become, in the full sense of the word, His Body the Church.

The disciples were about to pass through another period of transition which would result in a new and permanent relationship with Christ. The first transition had taken place during the three days when our Lord's body lay in the tomb. At first, the Apostles had followed Christ as a Man among men. That relationship came to an end in His death. During Eastertide, He appeared to them from time to time in His Risen Body, showing "himself alive after his passion by many infallible proofs." This form of His Self-manifestation was now to give way to the third. His followers were not to be dependent on intermittent Resurrection Appearances for their knowledge of Him. He willed to make Himself more readily accessible than that. He abides with us in word and sacraments until the end of time. On the Apostles He built His Church and "the gates of hell shall not prevail against it."

Accordingly, He bade them tarry in Jerusalem until they were "endued with power from on high." They were to await the promise of the Father of which He had told them. "For John truly baptized with water; but ye shall be baptized with the Holy Ghost not many days hence." Still they did not understand. "Lord, wilt thou at this time restore again the kingdom to Israel?" This question shows that they thought in terms of an earthly kingdom and the exaltation of the Jewish nation. That idea died slowly in their minds because it had so long been associated with the messianic hope. Our Lord did not even attempt to clarify their minds further on this point. He merely told them it was not for them to know the times or the seasons which the Father hath put in His own power. Time and the circumstances of future events would reveal the answer to them.

What our Lord was chiefly concerned to drive home to them was that other truth, considered in the preceding chapter, which their question showed they had not grasped. "Wilt thou at this time restore?" they had asked. The implication clearly was that they expected Him to do something further independently of them. But from now on, they were to be His agents. "Ye shall receive power, after that the Holy Ghost is come upon you: and ye shall be witnesses unto me both in Jerusalem, and in all Judea, and in Samaria, and unto the uttermost part of the earth." Those words, as we have seen, were the constantly recurring theme of the great Forty Days. They expressed the hardest and most important truth that the Apostles had to learn, that henceforth they were to be the Church, the Body through which Christ would continue to speak and act on earth.

In order to make them understand that they were no longer to expect Him to appear on earth in His Risen Body, He led them out to the Mount of Olives near Bethany and, after He had blessed them, "He was taken up; and a cloud received him out of their sight." There are many today who find it hard to believe in the Ascension. For, they argue, we know that the celestial arrangements presupposed in it are not correct. The sky is not a vast dome with heaven on top of it. Where did our Lord go when He was taken up?

This objection is rather silly. Our Lord was trying to convey a spiritual truth to the Apostles, not to give them a lesson in astronomy. Christ expressed Himself in terms of their thought-world for the same reason that He spoke to them in Aramaic. It was the only language they understood. But even if our Lord were to express the truth of the Ascension in terms of the Einstein universe, it is difficult to see how He could have done so in any other way than that He employed. He wanted His disciples to realize that His Risen Body was leaving the earth to take its place at the right hand of God. How else could He have given that note of finality?

It would not have been enough simply to disappear. All the other Resurrection Appearances had terminated in that way. That would have left the disciples expecting Him to return as He had before. It would not have done for Him to walk away from them over the brow of the hill. That would have given the impression that He was still roaming the earth. He could not die a second time, for one of the essential characteristics of His Risen Body is that it is beyond death. How could He express the teaching He had to give except by taking His Body either up into the air or down into the earth? Today, in spite of all our modern astronomy, we continue to think of heaven as up and hell as down. Thus the appropriate gesture by which to show that He was finally parted from us, as far as the visibility of His Resurrection Body is concerned, is still to be "carried up into heaven."

The Ascension reveals the destiny which God has pre-

pared for men. Jesus remains incarnate. He did not take
our human nature merely to lay it aside again either at
death or after He had demonstrated the Resurrection. He
united it to Himself permanently. He has raised it to the
right hand of God, which is a figurative way of saying that
man in Christ has been given the place of highest honor,
has been taken up into the Godhead itself.

Our Lord's humanity is united to ours by ties of blood.
There is an interrelationship on the natural level between
all members of the human race. In most instances, it may
be very distant and impossible to trace, but we are all off-
shoots of the same family tree. Through Mary, Jesus is one
of the human family. If we may picture mankind as a
triangle, then our Lord's human nature is its apex. At the
Ascension, He was raised up into the very heart of God.
This is, as it were, the entering wedge through which the
rest of the triangle can follow, if it so wills. The only
alternative is to break off from Him.

Thus Christ is, as He proclaimed Himself to be, a potentially divisive influence. "Think not that I am come to send
peace on earth: I came not to send peace, but a sword. For
I am come to set a man at variance against his father, and
the daughter against her mother, and the daughter-in-law
against her mother-in-law. And a man's foes shall be they
of his own household." Our Lord does not want to produce
conflict. But the salvation He offers must be freely accepted
or rejected. Men must choose; they must take sides. Since
all the difference between heaven and hell is involved in the
choice, hostility inevitably results as long as the two groups
live in the same society. The Christian, if he is faithful to
his Master, will not start the conflict, except in so far as his

uprightness itself is an affront to worldly selfishness and his occasional denunciation of sin and call to repentance is an offense to those who will not repent. But the world will hate him as it hated Christ and will seek to restrain and destroy him. Then the Christian's answer should be to suffer patiently and forgivingly. This is the basic technique of Christian warfare. It alone will achieve its object of winning souls to Christ.

Those who choose Christ and die faithful to Him will enter with Him into the glory which has been prepared. The Ascension teaches us that there should be no limit to human aspirations toward God. If we become servants of Christ, He calls us friends. From Him we "have received the Spirit of adoption whereby we cry, Abba, Father." "Behold, what manner of love the Father hath bestowed upon us, that we should be called the sons of God: and such we are." "If children, then heirs; heirs of God, and joint-heirs with Christ; if so be that we suffer with him, that we may be also glorified together." In Christ, we are to receive the highest honor; we are to be placed at God's right hand.

Herein we see the innate dignity of man. Human nature is capable of being the vehicle of the love of the Blessed Trinity. One of the ways in which the Son expresses His love of the Father is through His human nature. He did so on earth in His life of worship and obedience. He crowned that life with the Sacrifice of Calvary. Now risen and ascended, He continues to pour forth through His glorified manhood His eternal love. The Father looks lovingly on Him and cries, "This is my beloved Son, in whom I am well pleased."

We, united to Him by the Spirit, who is God dwelling in our hearts and loving the Son by integrating us into Him, participate in the Son's adoration of the Father. Our prayer and worship here in this world is a continuation through His Body the Church of the love He formerly expressed in His human nature. The voice which praises God through our voices is the Voice of Christ. The love which ascends through the aspiration of our hearts is the love of His Sacred Heart. The sacrifice which we re-present on our altar is His Sacrifice on the cross. "For as often as ye eat this bread, and drink this cup, ye do shew the Lord's death till He come."

When He does come to each of us at the moment of death, if He finds us abiding in Him, He takes us to Himself. "Beloved, now are we the sons of God, and it doth not yet appear what we shall be: but we know that, when he shall appear, we shall be like him; for we shall see him as he is." After having been cleansed of the dross of sin and made pure in heart, we shall see the Father face to face through the eyes of His Beloved Son. Finally, at the Last Day, our bodies shall rise and we shall receive them "fashioned like unto his glorious body." We shall continue for all eternity to be a channel through which the Father, Son, and Holy Ghost love each other.

Meanwhile "we have a great high priest, that is passed into the heavens, Jesus the Son of God . . . Wherefore he is able also to save them to the uttermost that come unto God by him, seeing he ever liveth to make intercession for them." We are remembered before God day and night. Christ our Brother prays constantly for us. He is the Good Shepherd who "calleth his own sheep by name." "I pray for them: I pray not for the world, but for them which thou hast given me; for they are thine . . . Those that thou gavest me I have kept, and none of them is lost, but the son of perdition"—that is, anyone who prefers to be a child of the devil rather than a son of God. But if we have chosen Christ, how confidently we may depend on Him who prays for us, "Father, I will that they also, whom thou hast given me, be with me where I am; that they may behold my glory, which thou hast given me: for thou lovedst me before the foundation of the world."

Within the heart of God there beats a human heart. The knowledge of that makes it so much easier to approach Him. He is a God of tremendous majesty, of righteousness and holiness. But through the experience of His human nature, He is also a God of infinite sympathy. He knows what is in man for He *is* Man. "He hath borne our griefs, and carried our sorrows." He knows how it feels to be hungry and weary, to be lonely and overburdened, to be slandered and misquoted, to be ridiculed and rejected, to be wounded and defeated. His cherished hopes have faded before His eyes. His proffered love has been spurned. He has died of a broken heart. "We have not an high priest which cannot be touched with the feeling of our infirmities; but was in all points tempted like as we are, yet without sin." Therefore we can "come boldly unto the throne of grace, that we may obtain mercy, and find grace to help in time of need." We know that we can conquer through Christ. "For in that he himself hath suffered being tempted, He is able to succour them that are tempted."

The disciples sensed something of this significance of the Ascension at the moment when Christ was taken up into heaven. For this reason, they felt none of the grief of Calvary at His parting from them. They realized that He had but gone before to prepare a place for them, remembering His promise, "I, if I be lifted up from the earth, will draw all men unto me." They expected Him to send them another Comforter who would keep them in touch with Him. Finally, they hoped that, as the "two men . . . in white apparel" informed them, "This same Jesus, which is taken up from you into heaven, shall so come in like manner as ye have seen him go into heaven." Therefore, as the Church puts it in one of the antiphons for the Feast of the Ascension: "While they looked stedfastly toward heaven as he went up, they said, Alleluia."

They "returned to Jerusalem with great joy: and were continually in the temple, praising and blessing God." In obedience to Christ's command to tarry in the Holy City, they abode in the Upper Room, where they "all continued with one accord in prayer and supplication." After ten days, the promise of the Father was fulfilled. On the Church the Holy Spirit descended as a rushing mighty wind and in cloven tongues of fire. "They were all filled with the Holy Ghost, and began to speak with other tongues, as the Spirit gave them utterance."

The impact of the gift of the Spirit on the Apostles was overwhelming. They reeled out of the house into the public square. Their joy, their sense of exuberant power made them act as if they were intoxicated. But even in the moment of their wildest excitement, they were impelled by missionary zeal. A desire to share with others what they had received, to win men to Christ, burned in their hearts. Peter mounted a rostrum to address the astonished crowd which had quickly assembled. He assured them that the disciples were not drunk with wine—it was only nine o'clock in the morning, too early for that. Thus opened the first Christian sermon!

Peter explained that the prophecy of Joel had been fulfilled. The Spirit of God had been poured forth upon man. "And it shall come to pass, that whosoever shall call on the name of the Lord shall be saved." Peter then proceeded to proclaim the Gospel, the Good News that God had raised Jesus from the dead and made Him "both Lord and Christ." So convincing was Peter's sermon and so infectious was the Apostles' fervor, that those who heard "were pricked in their heart" and asked, "Men and brethren, what shall we do?" They were told, "Repent, and be baptized everyone of you in the name of Jesus Christ for the remission of sins, and ye shall receive the gift of the Holy Ghost." "The same day there were added unto them about three thousand souls. And they continued stedfastly in the Apostles' doctrine and fellowship and in breaking of bread, and in prayers."

In this manner, the Church burst forth into the world. For a while, like a mountain stream near its source, it forged ahead with great rapidity, bounding over the rocks and sparkling in the sun. Many converts were made and the ecstatic manifestations of the Spirit continued. After a time, however, these began to die out. A quieter, more regular, more dependable operation of the Spirit took their place. This was as it should be, and the attempt on the part of certain members of the Church to perpetuate the more emotional signs of the Spirit by artificial stimulation were disastrous. Inspiration gave way to frenzy and the ecstatics became centers of heresy and schism. This danger was recognized early by the Church leaders. In the middle of the first century St. Paul, though he did not repudiate the charismatic gifts which he himself shared, insisted that intelligible prophesying was better than speaking with unknown tongues, and he urged people to seek the still more excellent gift of charity. St. John, toward the end of the century, issued a solemn warning, "Beloved, believe not every spirit, but try the spirits whether they are of God."

In the second century, persecution forced the Church underground. But it continued to flow on, fed by hidden springs. When it emerged at last, it engulfed the Roman Empire. It absorbed and swept into its current the Germanic tribes which overthrew the Empire. Irrigated by the life-giving waters of the Church, the medieval culture sprang up, flowered, and bore fruit.

Even when this fruit decayed, the river still flowed on. Unlike the civilizations which, in the course of history, either have tried to dam it up or have been nurtured by it, the Church is not of human origin. It is the work of God. It cannot be hindered by, nor is it dependent on, the man-made structures along its banks. At times, the debris of them may seem to pollute its waters. But like any living stream, it is able, as it flows along, to purify itself again. The most that human sin can do is to divert it from its original channel. When that happens, it simply cuts another, underground if need be, and moves invincible on its way.

The power of the Church may not always be apparent when it is viewed at just one point along its banks. This is particularly true today, since the Reformation has divided it into many little streams and since the silt of humanism muddies its waters. To appreciate its true grandeur, one must contemplate its entire length from source to mouth. Then one sees it flowing forth from God Incarnate, sweeping down through the centuries and emptying, at last, into the boundless ocean of God's love.

XV

The Heavens Opened

When they heard these things, they were cut to the heart, and they gnashed on him with their teeth. But he, being full of the Holy Ghost, looked up stedfastly into heaven, and saw the glory of God, and Jesus standing on the right hand of God, and said, Behold, I see the heavens opened, and the Son of man standing on the right hand of God. Then they cried out with a loud voice, and stopped their ears, and ran upon him with one accord, and cast him out of the city, and stoned him: and the witnesses laid down their clothes at a young man's feet, whose name was Saul. And they stoned Stephen, calling upon God, and saying, Lord Jesus, receive my spirit. And he kneeled down, and cried with a loud voice, Lord, lay not this sin to their charge. And when he said this, he fell asleep.

ACTS 7:54-60

Although the Ascension terminated the expectancy of the Resurrection Appearances, the Risen Christ showed Himself twice more to individuals while they were still in this life. Stephen, just before his death, "saw the glory of God, and Jesus standing on the right hand of God." Saul was confronted by Christ on the way to Damascus. There is no reason for doubting that these Appearances had the same objective reality as those which preceded them. In the Ascension, Christ took His Risen Body to heaven. There Stephen saw Him. Saul was met by a "light from heaven," which implies that Christ descended to Him. In his letter

189

to the Corinthians, Paul lists his experience as being on an equal footing with those of the Twelve. "Last of all he was seen of me also."

About the Appearance to Stephen not much needs to be said. It was fitting that the first Christian martyr should have seen the Risen Christ before he died. Our Lord encouraged him and placed the seal of approval on his faithfulness by giving him in this life a foretaste of what was to be his eternal joy in the life to come. Martyrdom is one of the greatest privileges which can be conferred on a Christian soul, the opportunity to give one's life for Him who gave His life for us. He who is faithful unto death passes through the final suffering into Christ's presence. Although the rest of the noble army of martyrs who have followed in Stephen's steps may not have seen the Lord Jesus in this world, they have been welcomed by Him with the same triumphant joy as they entered within the veil.

But martyrdom is also the supreme act of service to one's fellow-men. When it is accepted in the spirit of love and patience, it is the witness to Christ which most surely touches and converts the hearts of others. "The blood of the martyrs is the seed of the Church." The richest fruit of Stephen's death was the conversion of his chief accuser, the young man at whose feet the witnesses laid down their clothes, whose name was Saul. It is hard to avoid the impression that one of the reasons why the Risen Christ appeared to Stephen before his death was to effect Saul's conversion. Hence we shall consider this Appearance more in relation to Saul than to Stephen. As Mary Magdalene has been called the Apostle to the Apostles, since she brought to the Twelve the Glad Tidings of the Resurrection, so

Stephen might be called the Apostle to Paul. Stephen's testimony to the Appearance of the Risen Christ precipitated Saul into the final stages of his pre-conversion struggle.

We are accustomed to associate Saul's conversion with the Appearance of Christ to him on the Damascus Road, because these two events occurred at about the same time. But we should recognize that Saul's conversion preceded that Appearance. Saul had sinned in rejecting the Gospel and in persecuting the Church. As long as he remained in a state of rebellion, he could not see the Risen Lord. Christ had to wait until Saul was ready to receive Him before He could manifest Himself. The Appearance to Saul took place at the earliest moment possible, at the culmination of Saul's conversion; but it did not cause the conversion. God never overwhelms a soul by miracle. Our Lord specifically repudiated that technique when, in the wilderness, He rejected the temptation to win the allegiance of the Jews by floating gently down from a pinnacle of the Temple upheld by angelic hands. He seeks the willing surrender of human hearts, not their stunned acquiescence. He wants men to love Him, not to gape at Him. It was in the Appearance to Stephen that Christ touched the rebellious heart of Saul. The manifestation on the Damascus Road had a different purpose which we shall consider in the next chapter.

Saul's sin had caused an interruption in God's plans for him. From the beginning he was a chosen vessel of the Lord. As he wrote to the Galatians, he was separated from his mother's womb and called by God's grace to be the Apostle to the Gentiles. The circumstances of his early life were designed to equip him for his mission to them.

He was born and reared in a pagan land. From his father he inherited a citizenship in the Roman Empire. He spoke Greek fluently. His native Tarsus, "no mean city," was a provincial university town. There he absorbed, by osmosis, if not by actual study, much of Greek philosophy and culture. All this made it possible for him to preach the Gospel in terms that the Gentiles could understand. He was at home in their world of thought.

But before he could translate the Gospel for them he had to know it. Our Lord came as the Messiah, the Fulfilment of Israel's hope and destiny. To recognize Him and to understand His teaching in its original form, one had to be steeped in the religion of the Old Testament. Again, this necessary training was given to Saul. He was a Hebrew of the Hebrews. His parents belonged to the strictest sect of the Pharisees. In spite of their residence among the heathen, they were devotedly faithful to Jehovah. They kept the Law with fanatic zeal as a protection against the debasing pagan influences. These principles were built into their son's character. The keen mind with which he was endowed was given the best education available to Jews of his day. After his early schooling in the synagogs of Tarsus, he was sent to Jerusalem where he became the pupil of Gamaliel, a most learned rabbi who "taught according to the perfect manner of the Law of the fathers."

Saul's upbringing not only prepared him to understand and translate the Gospel message. It also planted in the forefront of his consciousness the problem which he more than anyone else was called upon to solve. He knew that the pagan civilization, magnificent as it was on the surface, was rotten at the core. It no longer satisfied the best of the Gentiles. Their hearts were hungry for salvation. The lofty monotheism and moral integrity of Judaism attracted them. Saul had seen them associating themselves with the synagogs of Tarsus, forming a fringe of so-called "God-fearers," who worshiped Jehovah and kept the Law as far as their Gentile customs would permit. Further than this they would not go. The ceremonial Law put excessive and unreasonable demands upon them. Here, then, was a rich harvest of souls to be reaped, if only the ceremonial requirements could be circumvented.

Yet this was precisely the one thing which could not be done under the Old Dispensation. Judaism was a religion of Law, with no provision for its adaptation to changing situations. This was the source of its strength and continuity. Those who kept the Law strictly were thereby made a people apart. Gentile influences could not penetrate through to them. They could live in the midst of a degenerate civilization and be impervious to it. Their own racial, moral, and religious integrity was preserved. By the same token, however, they had little effect on their environment. They did not convert the Gentiles. They excluded them.

These elements in Saul's education, necessary as they were to his vocation, nevertheless prevented him from becoming one of our Lord's early followers. Since he does not mention having seen Christ before the crucifixion, it is probable that he was not in Palestine during our Lord's public ministry. But even if he had been, he could never have been integrated into the fellowship of the first disciples. Saul was Greek-speaking, city-bred, a budding scholar, a strict Pharisee. The Twelve were Galilean peas-

ants, of great devotion but little learning, and most of
them had been disciples of John the Baptist whom the
Pharisees repudiated. Saul would have had to step completely out of character in order to share with Christ the
wanderings through the Galilean hills and the journeyings
back and forth across the lake.

Saul and the original disciples each had a different contribution to make to the establishment of the Church. The
Twelve were able to accompany our Lord during the public ministry and to receive His teaching from His lips.
But the factors which suited them for this work rendered
them incapable of grasping some of the implications of
the Gospel. Their horizon was limited to Palestine. They
assumed without question that they would go on being
devout Jews for the rest of their lives. It never occurred
to them that the Gentiles would want to become followers
of Christ without first becoming Jews, still less that it
was Christ's will that they should. They noted and re-
called His disputes with the Pharisees about the minutiae
of the Law, but they did not infer from them that the
ceremonial requirements of the Old Dispensation had been
abrogated.

Saul saw the inevitability of this inference as soon as he
heard the Gospel. Having lived with the Gentiles all his
life, he tested our Lord's teaching against the background
of his own experience. He concluded, correctly, that it
destroyed the foundations of that Jewish exclusiveness
which had been the means of preserving the Israelites from
absorption into the surrounding pagan culture. Our Lord's
disputes with the Pharisees were not quibbles on minor
points of the Law. They enunciated a new and revolution-

ary principle, that charity took precedence over the Law. Saul knew that, were such charity to be shown to the Gentiles, the defenses which the Law set up against them would speedily be infiltrated. Clearly, Christ did not consider salvation to be the exclusive prerogative of Israel. He had predicted that "many shall come from the east and west, and shall sit down with Abraham, and Isaac, and Jacob, in the kingdom of heaven. But the children of the kingdom shall be cast out into outer darkness." Saul sensed at once that there was an inherent incompatibility between the Gospel and the pharisaical conception of the Law.

This insight was also part of Saul's preparation for his vocation. Eventually, it was to become in his hands the battering-ram with which he would knock down "the middle wall of partition" between Jew and Greek. That was to be his unique contribution to the spread of Christianity. But his perception of the hostility between the Gospel and Jewish exclusiveness was at first a stumbling-block to his acceptance of Christ. It was bound to be, and it was right that it should. The Old Covenant was God's holy Law. Its value as a means of keeping the Jews faithful to Jehovah had been demonstrated over centuries of experience. No devout Jew would be justified in casting it aside lightly. Before Saul could accept the Gospel, he had to assure himself that Christ had the authority to change the old Law, that He was God's Agent with a higher commission than that which had been given to Moses, and that the freedom of the Gospel and the Law of love would not precipitate a degeneration to pagan standards, but would raise both Gentiles and Jews to a higher moral and spiritual level.

It was difficult for Saul to comprehend these staggering truths. But we must not conclude that it was impossible for him to arrive at them without first rejecting the Gospel and persecuting the infant Church. The latter course of action involved definite and deliberate sin. God never wills human sin, nor does He suffer a man to be tempted above what he is able to resist. We must assume, therefore, that, strong and understandable as was Saul's temptation to reject Christ, with the temptation God also made a way to escape, that Saul might be able to bear it. What that way was we can only guess. But we have a hint. Gamaliel, whom God appointed as Saul's teacher in the old Law, advocated an attitude of watchful waiting and suspended judgment in regard to Christianity, lest by opposing it they "be found even to fight against God." If Saul had heeded this advice, would he not have been led, slowly but irresistibly, by the logic of events and by the power of our Lord's love manifest in the Church, to accept the truth that Jesus is very Christ?

Saul, however, chose to disregard Gamaliel's warning. In this he sinned, and thereby postponed Christ's Appearance to him. He refused to accept the Gospel precisely because he was so attracted by it. His loyalty to the old Law had brought him no peace of mind. Under the strict pharisaic interpretation, salvation depended on keeping the whole Law perfectly. "Cursed is everyone that continueth not in all things which are written in the book of the Law to do them." Saul was honest enough with himself to admit that he had failed in this respect in the past, and that, day by day, in spite of his best efforts, the score against him was growing. There was no way in which this debt could be paid. Since perfect obedience to the Law was required in the first instance, there was no way to make reparation for past failures. All one could do was to offer sacrifices of atonement. As these were mere ritual acts, they did little to ease the conscience of the morally sensitive Saul. His devotion to the Law convinced him that he stood condemned by it.

Consequently, he envied the Christians' certainty of salvation through Christ; he coveted their hope, their joy, and the enthusiasm with which they were able to abandon themselves to the service of God. Yet, although in his heart he yearned for their peace and in his mind he perceived at least dimly that this came from their trust, not in the works of the Law, but in the mercy of God, nevertheless he rejected Christ and clung to the traditions of his fathers. His pride would not suffer him to surrender himself utterly into our Lord's hands.

His sin was his own peculiar brand of gloomy, puritanical Pharisaism. It was not the complacent self-satisfaction of the Pharisee in the Temple who thanked God that he was not as other men are and boasted his faithfulness in keeping the Law. Saul had faced and admitted his shortcomings. He knew that he stood accursed by the Law and expected no reward. He counted himself irreparably lost. But if he could not save himself by his own efforts, he preferred not to be saved at all. He would not throw himself on the divine mercy. Instead, he would get back at God, as it were, by upholding the Law that condemned him and by sacrificing himself to God's justice.

No doubt there were secondary forms of pride that encouraged his rejection of Christ. He, a learned doctor of the Law, was unwilling to become a Christian neophyte and to seek instruction at the feet of Galilean peasants. His position of prominence and influence with the Jewish authorities, his hopes of a brilliant career as a rabbi and member of the Sanhedrin, were hard to surrender. But the deepest and most impelling motive was this acme of Pharisaism, the determination to prove himself holier than God by accepting without protest his unavoidable condemnation and by glorifying the God who had tricked him into it.

Here is the source of his fanatic zeal against the Church. Unwilling to surrender to the peace which the Christians had found in Christ, he was determined that they should not enjoy it, either. He suppressed his attraction for it by treating it as an enticement of the devil, designed to lure him from his self-chosen course of heroic self-immolation. Christianity must be destroyed, discredited at all cost, to prove that Saul was right. He threw himself against the Church in a violent attack, dragging the Christians before the magistrates and demanding that the maximum penalties be inflicted upon them.

But the long-suffering Christ would not let His chosen servant go. He pursued Saul relentlessly, revealing His love through the suffering members of His Body the Church. No amount of torment could wring from them a denial of their Master or a counterattack on Saul. They bore it all with humble patience and forgiving love. This goaded Saul to more frantic efforts.

The climax came when Saul hailed Stephen before the Jewish tribunal. There Stephen, instead of cowering before his judges, launched into a sermon which concluded with a

denunciation of them for having not kept the Law themselves and for being "betrayers and murderers" of Christ.
Such a defense was hardly calculated to ingratiate Stephen
with the authorities. "They gnashed on him with their
teeth" and the surrounding mob echoed their sentiments.

Suddenly a marked change came over the prisoner. He
raised his eyes. A supernatural radiance was reflected in
them. "Behold," he cried, "I see the heavens opened, and
the Son of man standing on the right hand of God." Saul,
as he watched, could not avoid the conviction that Stephen
saw Someone where, for Saul, there was no one to be seen.
Saul's hatred against Stephen overflowed. He had no difficulty in persuading the mob to fall upon Stephen and to
drag him off to the place of execution without awaiting
the formality of his being condemned and sentenced by
the court.

Stephen was thrown into the pit and the stones began
to rain down upon him. But he knelt there unheeding, his
eyes still fixed on his beloved Master who smiled upon him
from the Throne of God. "Lord Jesus, receive my spirit."
Saul closed his eyes to shut out the spectacle of the manifest
reality of Stephen's experience. Whereupon, on Saul's ears
fell those gracious words which made him quiver with
impotent rage, "Lord, lay not this sin to their charge."
How could one defeat a man who died like that?

The immediate result of this episode was to send Saul,
"yet breathing out threatenings and slaughter against the
disciples of the Lord," to the High Priest to get letters to
the synagogs of Damascus in order that he might arrest
the Christians there and "bring them bound unto Jerusalem." That, however, was to be the death-throe of his

struggle against the Gospel. The Risen Christ had penetrated to Saul's heart. His love could not be resisted much
longer. Before Saul ever reached Damascus, he would surrender to that love. It was characteristic of God's dealings
with men that our Lord had approached and conquered
the rebellious Saul, not by appearing to him directly, but
by reaching out to him through Stephen, a faithful member of His Body the Church.

Saul had not seen our Lord die on Calvary. But he saw
Stephen die with the same words of forgiveness on his lips.
Thus Stephen filled up that which was behind of the afflictions of Christ in his flesh, revealing anew the saving power
of the Cross, drawing Saul to the Master's feet.

XVI

Born Out of Due Time

And last of all he was seen of me also, as of one born out of due time. For I am the least of the apostles, that am not meet to be called an apostle, because I persecuted the Church of God. But by the grace of God I am what I am.

I CORINTHIANS 15:8-10.

And as he journeyed, he came near Damascus: and suddenly there shined round about him a light from heaven: and he fell to the earth, and heard a voice saying unto him, Saul, Saul, why persecutest thou me? And he said, Who art thou, Lord? And the Lord said, I am Jesus whom thou persecutest: it is hard for thee to kick against the pricks. And he trembling and astonished said, Lord, what wilt thou have me to do? And the Lord said unto him, Arise, and go into the city, and it shall be told thee what thou must do. And the men which journeyed with him stood speechless, hearing a voice, but seeing no man.

ACTS 9:3-7.

And it came to pass, that, as I made my journey, and was come nigh unto Damascus about noon, suddenly there shone from heaven a great light round about me. And I fell unto the ground, and heard a voice saying unto me, Saul, Saul, why persecutest thou me? And I answered, Who art thou, Lord? And he said unto me, I am Jesus of Nazareth, whom thou persecutest. And they that were with me saw indeed the light, and were afraid; but they heard not the voice of him that spake to me. And I said, What shall I do, Lord? And the Lord said unto me, Arise, and go into Damascus; and there it shall be told thee of all things which are appointed for thee to do.

*And when I could not see for the glory of that light, being
led by the hand of them that were with me, I came into Damascus. And one Ananias, a devout man according to the law, having a good report of all the Jews which dwelt there, came unto
me, and stood, and said unto me, Brother Saul, receive thy
sight. And the same hour I looked up upon him. And he said,
The God of our fathers hath chosen thee, that thou shouldest
know his will, and see that Just One, and shouldest hear the
voice of his mouth. For thou shalt be his witness unto all men
of what thou hast seen and heard. And now why tarriest thou?
arise, and be baptized, and wash away thy sins, calling on the
name of the Lord.*   ACTS 22:6-16.

*Whereupon as I went to Damascus with authority and com-
mission from the chief priests, at midday, O king, I saw in the
way a light from heaven, above the brightness of the sun,
shining round about me and them which journeyed with me.
And when we were all fallen to the earth, I heard a voice speaking unto me, and saying in the Hebrew tongue, Saul, Saul, why
persecutest thou me? it is hard for thee to kick against the
pricks. And I said, who art thou, Lord? And he said, I am
Jesus whom thou persecutest. But rise, and stand upon thy feet:
for I have appeared unto thee for this purpose, to make thee a
minister and a witness both of these things which thou hast
seen, and of those things in the which I will appear unto thee;
delivering thee from the people, and from the Gentiles, unto
whom now I send thee, to open their eyes, and to turn them
from darkness to light, and from the power of Satan unto God,
that they may receive forgiveness of sins, and inheritance among
them which are sanctified by faith that is in me.*

ACTS 26:12-18.

When Saul set out from Jerusalem, his heart was filled
with hatred against the Christians. As he neared Damascus,

the Risen Christ appeared to him. Between those two events Saul's conversion took place.

The journey was long and slow. It forced Saul to face certain questions which he had hitherto been escaping by plunging himself into his frenzied activity of persecution. Although the purpose of his visit to Damascus was to extend the range of his operations, there was nothing he could actually do about them until he arrived. As he trudged along the dusty road, he had time to reflect. Probably, at first, he succeeded in occupying his mind with his plans for the Damascus campaign. But, eventually, that subject exhausted itself. He could no longer postpone asking himself whether in persecuting the Church he was doing right.

The scene of Stephen's martyrdom haunted him. Was Stephen's claim, that he saw the Lord Jesus, false? Whence then came that triumphant joy which made him indifferent to the torrent of stones which were falling upon him? Whence the confidence with which he surrendered his soul to Christ? Whence the power to forgive his persecutors? Could this be the work of the devil? The more Saul tried to assure himself that it was, the less confident he became. He could not deny the unfavorable contrast between his own blind fury and Stephen's patient and loving constancy. All the evidence was against Saul.

Yet if Christianity were not the work of the devil, there was but one alternative. Gamaliel's warning was justified. Saul was fighting against God. Again and again Saul rejected that conclusion. Again and again it returned with increasing force. Saul's pride insisted it could not be true. Saul could not be wrong. Moses could not be wrong.

The Law was God's decree; no man could change it. The Children of Israel were God's Chosen People. They must not be contaminated by the intrusion of the Gentiles. Cost what it would, they must remain faithful to Jehovah.

Meanwhile, Saul's reasoning powers and his knowledge of the Old Testament were leading him along another path. The pharisaic concept of the Law was not the only tradition in the Jewish religion. It was, in fact, a rather recent school of thought. The Scriptures were full of promises that eventually all men should know and serve Jehovah. These promises were associated with the coming of the Messiah and the outpouring of the Spirit upon all flesh. The Christians claimed that had happened already. Their actions were evidence that the claim was true.

But their Messiah had been crucified. This was contrary to the Jewish expectations of what would happen when Christ came. Or was it? Isaiah had prophesied, "He is despised and rejected of men; a Man of sorrows, and acquainted with grief. . . . He was wounded for our transgressions . . . He is brought as a lamb to the slaughter . . . He was taken from prison and from judgment . . . He made his grave with the wicked." Had not Jesus fulfilled that prophecy to the letter? Again, the Psalmist had predicted, "They pierced my hands and my feet: I may tell all my bones: they stand staring and looking upon me. They part my garments among them, and cast lots upon my vesture." It was a perfect description of what had happened on Calvary.

Saul could not refrain from considering Christ's claims seriously. What would be the practical result of accepting them? The destruction of Israel? As the Pharisees con-

ceived it, yes. But were Jesus' standards lower than those
of the Pharisees? Jesus had accused the Pharisees of substi-
tuting meticulous concern over minute requirements of
the Law for sincere love of God and man. Saul could not
deny the justice of the charge. Jesus had pointed out how
the Pharisees stood in a bargaining relationship with God,
how they demanded His favor because they had kept the
letter of the Law. Jesus called them to repentance, to the
recognition of their utter dependence on God, to a more
generous self-oblation. Saul's own experience convinced
him that Jesus was right. He could not bargain with God
for, in fact, he had not kept the Law. He had found it impossible to keep it. "The good that I would I do not: but
the evil which I would not, that I do." He could not save
himself. If he were saved at all, it would be only because
he had thrown himself on God's mercy. This Jesus had
promised him. Should he not accept it?

If Saul admitted that Jesus was God's Messiah establishing a New Covenant with Israel, then the arguments he
had used against Christ became arguments against continuing under the Old Dispensation. The works of the Law
had not succeeded in saving man. They were too heavy a
yoke for man to bear. Instead of a blessing, they had become a curse. But Christ, by dying on the cross, had Himself redeemed man "from the curse of the Law, being made
a curse for us: (for it is written, Cursed is everyone that
hangeth on a tree) that the blessing of Abraham might
come on the Gentiles through Jesus Christ; that we might
receive the promise of the Spirit through faith." The
New Covenant offered salvation to both Jew and Gentile,
not on the basis of what they had done for God, "for all

have sinned, and come short of the glory of God," but by a humble, penitent, loving surrender into Christ's hands. In Him, they would be saved. In Him, they would find what the Law never gave, the power to do God's will. Obedience to God's commandments and precepts would still be required, for to love is to obey. That obedience would be costly. Saul himself had made too many Christians suffer for their faith to have any doubts about that. But he also knew that those disciples of the Lord Jesus had found a source of strength that enabled them to persevere to the end in constancy and love. Theirs was an unconquerable stedfastness.

The acceptance of Jesus as the Messiah would not involve a total repudiation of the Law and traditions, in which Saul had been nurtured, which he loved. Rather, they would be raised to a higher spiritual fruitfulness in Christ. Had He not said, "Think not that I am come to destroy the Law, or the prophets: I am not come to destroy, but to fulfil?" The negative, exclusive elements of the pharisaical concept of the Law would be done away. But even they would not be wholly repudiated. They had served a purpose in God's plan. To the Jews He had committed the revelation of Himself as the One and Holy God. This was to prepare them for His coming among them as a Member of their race. This revelation had to be preserved from contamination by the surrounding polytheistic religions. The Law, with its exclusive barriers, had accomplished that. But now the Messiah had come and at least a few had recognized Him. The need for exclusiveness was past. The time had arrived for a world-wide mission to bring all men to the feet of Christ.

Since Saul has left us no record of his process of thought, we cannot be sure that the above reconstruction is accurate. It was the position he held at the time he wrote his Epistles. There is no reason to doubt that he reached it in substance as he walked to Damascus. Only something like it could have resolved his struggle against Christ. For just as we may be certain that our Lord did not startle Saul into submission by thrusting Himself on him uninvited, so we may confidently affirm that Saul's submission to Christ was based on three considerations: first, that Jesus was God's Messiah instituting a new relationship between God and man; second, that the New Covenant was the completion not the abandonment of the Old; and third, that all men could become members of the new and glorified Israel.

Saul was now ready to surrender to Christ. He repented his sin in persecuting the Church. He yielded to his longing for salvation and peace. Immediately, he was suffused in a light from heaven. "Saul, Saul, why persecutest thou me?" "Who art thou, Lord?" "I am Jesus whom thou persecutest: it is hard for thee to kick against the pricks." "Lord, what wilt thou have me to do?" And Saul lay on the ground, blind in body but no longer in soul, rejoicing that the bitter struggle had ended in his glorious defeat.

If, as we maintain, the Appearance of Christ to Paul was not in order to convert him, what then was its purpose? The Risen Christ Himself answers our question. Paul reports Him as having said, "I have appeared unto thee for this purpose, to make thee a minister and a witness both of these things which thou hast seen, and of those things in which I will appear unto thee; delivering thee from the people, and from the Gentiles, unto whom I now send thee, to open their eyes, and to turn them from darkness to light, and from the power of Satan unto God, that they may receive forgiveness of sins, and inheritance among them which are sanctified by faith that is in me." Our Lord appeared to Paul to confer on him the rank of an Apostle, that is, one who has seen the Risen Christ, and to commission him to carry the Gospel to the Gentiles.

In order that Paul might fulfil his vocation to bring the Gentiles into the Church, he had to be an Apostle on an equal footing with the Twelve. We have seen how they, being natives of Palestine, never envisioned that the Gentiles were to be admitted without first becoming Jews. They were bound to question Paul's interpretation of the Gospel. To persuade them that it was right, he had to be vested with the same authority which they had. At the height of the controversy on the subject, he would have to be able to claim that he was "an Apostle, not of men, neither by man, but by Jesus Christ, and God the Father, who raised him from the dead."

Therefore, we can safely conclude that our Lord intended from the first to appear to Paul. If Saul had not sinned, the Appearance would have occurred sooner, perhaps, and under different circumstances. This seems to be what Paul had in mind when he wrote that he was "born out of due time." That he was thinking about his birth as an Apostle, and that the delay was caused by his sin, is clear from the verses that follow that phrase. "For I am the least of the apostles, that am not meet to be called an apostle, because I persecuted the Church of God. But by the grace of God I am what I am." In spite of Paul's sin, Christ had appeared to him and sent him to convert the Gentiles.

Although he received that commission from Christ on the Damascus Road, Paul was not permitted at once to put it into execution. He had first to pass through the ordinary process of Christian nurture. He was baptized by Ananias like the humblest neophyte. After his preliminary testimony to Christ in the synagogs of Damascus, he went to Arabia for a period of prayer and retreat. Returning to Damascus, he worked there for three years, after which he went to Jerusalem, where he was received by Peter, and James, the Lord's brother. There followed another period of retirement and obscurity, this time in his native Tarsus, before he was called by Barnabas to Antioch. Only after this long preparation was Paul given the opportunity to exercise his Apostolate and to make the practical application of the truth on which his conversion had turned.

Furthermore, his authority, given as it had been by Christ, had also to be confirmed by the Church. Paul again journeyed to Jerusalem. He presented his credentials and justified his Gentile policy before the "pillars" of the Church—James, the Lord's brother, Peter, and John. They recognized his Apostleship by giving him the "right hand of fellowship," and endorsed his policy by committing the Gospel of the uncircumcision into his hands. Even this, however, was not enough. Conservative members of the Jerusalem Church subsequently raised objections. James seems to have been swayed by them, and even Peter wavered. The Apostolic Council was called and settled the question in Paul's favor. Thus Christ through the Church confirmed His private revelation to Paul, who thenceforth devoted his life to establishing the Gentiles in the Gospel.

Paul has been called the Apostle of Unity. He made the

Jews and Greeks one in Christ. "There is neither Jew nor Greek, there is neither bond nor free, there is neither male nor female: for ye are all one in Christ Jesus." To the religion of the Old Testament, interpreted in the light of the Gospel, he added the philosophical and moral speculations of the Greeks. Using the superb system of communication of the Roman Empire, he planted Christianity in many places and bound the local congregations into an ordered whole. In this way, he combined the best of three cultures, Hebrew religion, Greek thought, and Roman organization, uniting them in Christ, and laying the foundations of Christian theology and of the world-wide Church.

In this day, when Christendom is so sadly divided, we have much to learn from Paul. Like him before his conversion, we are likely, through devotion to a partial revelation, to reject the fulness of the Gospel. Each of us has been nurtured in one of the many Christian sects. Every Christian group possesses some fragment, large or small, of the totality of Christian truth. No group possesses it all, though for centuries each has been claiming that it does and denying the truth of what some of the others hold. Hence, in the official position of each Christian body, there is to be found some positive truth and some negations of it. If we are content to remain as we are, we adopt the position of Saul the Pharisee. We hold tenaciously to a part of God's revelation. But instead of contributing it to a common understanding of the Gospel, we make it a basis of exclusiveness. Other Christians must agree with us or remain beyond the pale. Aspects of the Christian tradition which, if we accepted them, would undermine our attitude of superiority, are rejected with scorn and derision.

The road to truth and unity, as Saul discovered, lies in the opposite direction. It is God's will that all the fragments be gathered up and fitted together. Because we have all been raised in a partial Christian tradition, we all have much to learn. We should make a serious effort to comprehend the truths which are enshrined in other traditions and to see how they can be integrated with what we already hold. But it must be a true synthesis in which nothing is discarded on either side except our prejudices and negations.

We should be on guard against those who advocate a different course. Some, wearied by the quarrels which have disrupted Christendom for centuries and distressed by the weakness of a divided Church, propose a short-cut to unity. They ask us to cast aside the doctrines and practices over which controversies have raged, and to get together on the basis of what is left. Since there is hardly a dogma of the Faith or an element of the spiritual life which is not rejected by one or another Christian group, reunion along these lines would result in a common agreement to believe and to do nothing.

Another and even more dangerous proposal is that groups whose fragments of the truth coincide unite against those who hold a quite different position. This is the creed of Pan-Protestantism. Its ideal for the Church is to establish two hostile camps—Catholic and Protestant. How that could be called the "unity of the Spirit in the bond of peace" is hard to understand.

No, we must follow in the footsteps of Saul. We must repent our exclusiveness and rethink our prejudices. Then we shall discover that the elements of the Christian tradition which we have been repudiating most emphatically are just what we need to transform our narrow half-truths into a more fruitful comprehension of the Gospel. Without the inclusion of the Gentiles, which Saul feared would undermine men's faithfulness to God, Judaism, yes, and Jewish Christianity, would have remained a small, ineffectual, barren sect. We know that because it happened. There were some Jewish Christians who were never reconciled to the admission of the Gentiles. They formed a little eddy cut off from the main stream, which dried up in the second century.

Both Protestantism and Catholicism are in danger of the same fate if they remain hostile to each other. (We are using the term "Catholic" as a party and sect name, not in its true etymological sense of the universal Faith and practice which no modern division of Christendom has in its integrity.) Protestantism and Catholicism need each other. They stress different yet complementary elements in the full Gospel. Protestantism needs the authority, the discipline, the firm grasp on dogma and worship, the continuity with the past, which we associate with Catholicism. It, in turn, needs the emphasis on freedom, on individual responsibility, on moral integrity, on the daring quest for new insights into the truth and new applications of it to current problems, which characterize Protestantism at its best. Yet the Protestant tends to reject Catholic practices because he fears they will deprive him of his unfettered independence and contaminate his lofty isolation. The Catholic, in the smug security of his well-ordered worldwide organization, is inclined to sneer at the vagaries and confusion of Protestantism. Thereby both shut themselves out from the full and fruitful liberty of the sons of God.

What can the individual do? He can make an effort to glimpse something of the whole picture. He can study other Christian traditions, striving to see how the best in them can be combined with the best of what he has held before. If he does discover how some of the pieces fit, what then? Should he rush off and found a new sect incorporating them both? No. Again Paul shows us the way. As he went from his contact with the Risen Christ into Damascus and was baptized, so for us the first step will be to surrender ourselves to the new insight and make it a part of our own devotional lives. Perhaps, after years of prayer and humble service, like Paul, we may be called to help others make the same integration. If not, our prayers and sympathetic understanding of divergent traditions, our own living synthesis of them, will make a real contribution. If all Christians were making an honest effort to appreciate each other's point of view, we should be much nearer that great day when our Lord's own prayer will be realized, "That they may be one."

After centuries of a divided Christendom, no man can know what the fulness of the Gospel means. But our Lord knows, and His Mind is the Mind of the Church. Through the Holy Spirit, whom He has given us, He can and, if we let Him, He will, lead us into all truth. Until we arrive we cannot imagine what it will be like. Nevertheless, we would venture one prediction. Nothing which over the years has proved to be of positive spiritual value in any Christian tradition will be lost. Everything, from the papacy to lay participation in Church government, from Solemn High Mass to Wednesday Night Prayer Meeting, from devotions to the Mother of God to Quaker silence will find its place in the finished edifice. Some may be changed almost beyond recognition when their rough edges have been hewn off and the incrustation of sin has been chipped away. But all will be there when "the building fitly framed together groweth unto a holy temple in the Lord."

XVII

The Judgment

*He ascended into heaven, and sitteth on the right hand of God
the Father Almighty: from thence he shall come to judge
the quick and the dead.*

APOSTLES' CREED.

*And ascended into heaven, and sitteth on the right hand of
the Father: and he shall come again with glory, to judge both
the quick and the dead; whose Kingdom shall have no end.*

NICENE CREED.

*He ascended into heaven, he sitteth on the right hand of the
Father, God Almighty; from when he shall come to judge
the quick and the dead. At whose coming all men shall rise
again with their bodies, and shall give account for their own
works. And they that have done good shall go into life everlasting; and they that have done evil into everlasting fire. This
is the Catholic Faith, which except a man believe faithfully,
he cannot be saved.*

ATHANASIAN CREED.

You and I also shall see the Risen Christ. It may be that
we shall see Him before we die. For at the end of the world
"He shall come again with glory, to judge both the
quick and the dead." This article of the Creed would lead
us to believe that some men will still be alive at the time
of the Second Coming. There is always the possibility that

we shall be among them. Since we do not know the times or the seasons, the end of the world may be a million years hence; or it may occur tomorrow morning.

The early Church expected the Christian Dispensation to be of very short duration on earth. The disciples apparently understood some of our Lord's sayings to mean that the end of the world would come in their lifetimes. "Verily I say unto you, That there be some of them that stand here, which shall not taste of death, till they have seen the Kingdom of God come with power." This is a difficult passage to interpret. Presumably, since our Lord could hardly have been mistaken on this point, He was referring either to the manifestation of His Resurrection or to the establishment of the Church. But the Apostles and Evangelists tended to color His words with their own expectations of a speedy end. St. Paul seems to have shared this view. "Behold, I shew you a mystery; we shall not all sleep, but we shall all be changed, in a moment, in the twinkling of an eye, at the last trump."

Here is another marked difference between the Church of the first century and modern Christianity. We have settled into an attitude that this world will continue so far into the future that for all practical purposes we can ignore its eventual termination. To a degree, it is both inevitable and healthy that the sense of immediate anticipation should diminish as the years have passed by and the Second Coming has been deferred. It is hard to maintain an attitude of expecting it to occur at any moment after so many centuries. Yet we must never blind ourselves completely to the truth that it may happen at any time.

The beneficial consequence of the loss of expectancy is

that there is less danger of a wrong kind of otherworldliness which the first century Church had to combat. St. Paul's second letter to the Thessalonians is a warning against it. His first Epistle had said "that the Day of the Lord so cometh as a thief in the night." Some had inferred from that, apparently with the help of a forged letter purporting to come from St. Paul, that there was no point in working on earth any longer. The end was in sight. Why go on with jobs and other occupations? To correct that misinterpretation, St. Paul wrote again, assuring the Thessalonians that before the Second Coming there would be a "falling away first, and that man of sin be revealed, the son of perdition." In other words, the final termination would be preceded by a great outbreak of evil involving a persecution of the Church. Until that had happened, they should not expect the end to come.

These two concepts of the Last Day—first, that it would occur without warning and second, that it would be preceded by certain recognizable signs—run side by side through the New Testament. Our Lord Himself taught both. "The Kingdom of God cometh not with observation. . . . As the lightning cometh out of the east, and shineth even unto the west; so shall also the Son of man be." That emphasizes the unexpected element in the Second Coming. On the other hand, there is the passage, "For false Christs and false prophets shall rise, and shall shew signs and wonders, to seduce, if it were possible, even the elect. . . . In those days, after that tribulation, the sun shall be darkened, and the moon shall not give her light, and the stars of heaven shall fall. . . . And then shall they see the Son of man coming in the clouds with great power and

glory. . . . When ye shall see these things come to pass, know
that it is nigh, even at the doors." This clearly teaches that
there will be preliminary warnings of the approaching end.

No doubt, these seemingly contradictory statements will
be reconciled in the final dénouement. But since our Lord
did not indicate how it will be accomplished, we are not
to speculate on this question. We should simply hold both
the truths that the two predictions enshrine.

Our Lord points out the conclusion we are to draw from
the possible proximity of the end of the world. "Let your
loins be girded about, and your lights burning; and ye
yourselves like unto men that wait for their lord, when he
will return from the wedding; that when he cometh and
knocketh, they may open unto him immediately. Blessed are
those servants whom the lord when he cometh shall find
watching. . . . Be ye therefore ready also: for the Son of man
cometh at an hour when ye think not." St. Paul echoes
the same sentiment. "And that, knowing the time, that now
it is high time to awake out of sleep: for now is our salvation nearer than when we believed. The night is far spent,
the day is at hand."

The Day of the Lord will be a great and glorious day for
those who are ready to receive Him. For those who are not
ready, it will be a time of weeping and gnashing of teeth.
Christ will come to judge. His judgment will be just, merci-
ful, and loving; but it will be irrevocable. The souls who,
whatever their failings and sins, are holding fast to Him
in penitence and love will be saved. The souls who have
developed an ingrained habit of ignoring Christ, of living
for themselves, or of using the Christian religion as the
means of their own self-advancement, who, in short, are

refusing to give themselves to Christ, will be permitted to exist forever without Him. No one, of course, is ever tricked into hell. The souls there have all deliberately chosen it. But we must be on our guard against the attitude that we can reject Christ temporarily with the assurance that there will be plenty of time subsequently to repent and be saved.

This belief is fallacious on several counts. The deeper we go into sin, the harder it is to get out. The power to repent is not something we generate for ourselves; it is a gift of the Holy Spirit. There is a state of soul in which it becomes impossible to co-operate with the grace of penitence. That is the sin against the Holy Ghost for which our Lord said there is no forgiveness. We can never be sure when the deliberate indulgence in sin will precipitate us into that condition.

However, the clearest and most dramatic deterrent against temporizing with sin is the thought that the end may come even as we are in the act of committing it. We may be caught red-handed. If we find ourselves in that unfortunate predicament, we shall have no grounds for complaining that we have been treated unfairly. We have been warned repeatedly and distinctly that we must be ready at all times for the coming of Christ in judgment. Although, psychologically, the deferring of the end of the world has diminished our sense of expectancy, rationally it should have the opposite effect. Our salvation, after all, is nineteen hundred years nearer than when Paul believed. How short the remaining time is we cannot know, but at least it is that much shorter than it was in the first century.

Furthermore, the end of the world is not the only way

in which an individual is brought to the Judgment Seat of Christ. Each soul at death sees the Risen Lord and learns from that experience his eternal destiny. For the soul who dies in sin, it is an occasion of inconceivable despair, when the soul not only sees himself as he is in the sight of God, but also glimpses for a moment the overwhelming beauty and loveliness of Christ, from the enjoyment of which the soul by his sin has excluded himself forever. The realization and, inconsistently, the resentment of that loss will be the chief element in the interminable agony of hell.

If the end of the world seems remote, at least we cannot deny the fact that our natural death may occur at any moment. No second passes without some souls' plunging through the veil of death. Among them is a large percentage of children, of young men and women, of people in the prime of life. The next second it may be you or I.

The Church has always urged us to meditate often on death. There is nothing morbid, in the popular sense of the word, about the practice. Death for a Christian is not an experience to be dreaded or shunned. It is meant to be the moment when we enter into the fulfilment of our hope, when, at last, we enjoy what we have so long desired, when the Risen Christ appears to us in the fulness of His glory.

We should be looking forward to death. We should be as eager as St. John was for the coming of the Lord. There are only two possible reasons why we do not have this attitude. The first is ignorance of the Resurrection and all that it implies. This book has sought to do something to correct that deficiency. The second is unpreparedness for the accompanying judgment. The cure for that is to begin right now to prepare. The judgment cannot be escaped.

But through the infinite mercy of God we can be ready for it and we can receive a favorable verdict. If the event proves otherwise, we shall have no one to blame but ourselves. God has done all in His almighty power to win our love. He has died for us. If by refusing to meditate on death, we seek to escape the fact of judgment and to live our lives as though we did not have, in the near future, to look into the eyes of the Risen Christ, then we are rejecting His love. We are declaring, by actions that speak louder than words, that we are content to live forever without Him.

We shall be judged on the basis of our works. That does not mean that we shall be saved by our own efforts. Salvation depends solely on the merits of Christ. Our recognition of this and our surrender to Him in this life are the only grounds for Christian hope. Invincible ignorance alone can excuse the soul who has not accepted Christ. Only God can know when ignorance is truly invincible, and those who belong in that category will themselves be saved through the Atonement wrought on Calvary, even though on earth they had no opportunity of recognizing it. Christ is the one Portal to everlasting life. As He said, "I am the door: by me if any man enter in, he shall be saved." Those to whom that truth has been revealed must consciously knock at that Doorway. Those who, according to their lights, have actually sought it, but, through no fault of their own, have not known its name, shall also enter in by it. All who are saved shall be saved through Christ.

Knocking at the Door, however, involves more than lip-service. "Not everyone that saith unto me, Lord, Lord, shall enter into the Kingdom of heaven." Faith in Christ alone can save. But what is faith? An attitude of mind? A barren recognition of Christ which bears no fruit in daily living? St. James rightly asks, "What doth it profit, my brethren, though a man say he hath faith, and have not works? can faith save him?" He challenges such a man, "Shew me thy faith without thy works, and I will shew thee my faith by my works." The former demonstration cannot be made. For "faith, if it have not works, is dead."

Good works are the evidence of a living faith in the Risen Christ. No one can act on the belief that God became Man, went about doing good, gave His life on the cross, rose again from the dead and calls us into His Body the Church, without his life's being changed by that faith. Failure to act on that belief is to reject it. Acceptance of it demands a surrender to Christ which impels the believer to good works. Gratitude for the divine condescension in becoming Man and for the divine love revealed on Calvary must express itself in worship and praise. Recognition of how sin crucified Christ will cause the true believer to shun every occasion of temptation, to resist even "unto blood, striving against sin," and to grieve with a prompt and hearty penitence over any failure in love. The assured hope of the Resurrection will lead the soul to lift his heart fervently and frequently in prayer. Knowledge that one is a member of Christ's Body, the agent of His love, will make one diligent in the service of the Church; and since it is Christ who suffers in our brethren, fellow-members of Him, we shall do all in our power to feed and clothe and cheer them. Such works, outward and visible acts of devotion and mercy, are the sacramental expression of our faith. If they are lacking, we may know that there is no faith in us; we are dead in our sins.

A lively faith in the Risen Christ results in an earnest application to current duties here on earth. This is where the other emphasis in our Lord's teaching about the coming judgment applies. Although we must be ready for it at any moment, we must not let our expectancy rise to such a fever pitch that it causes us to shirk our present obligations. Christ has a work to do and a battle to win in and through us before we can pass on to glory. How long the battle will last we cannot know. The end, as we have seen, may come at any moment; and it probably will not await the time when we think our task is complete. Our concept of the work we have to do and the way in which it will be accomplished rarely coincides exactly with God's plans for us. Therefore, until we have clear indications that the end is at hand, we should keep struggling on, fulfilling our daily duties with whole-hearted zeal, leaving the future in God's hands. It is for Him to give the increase. Ours but to labor on in the assurance that "all things work together for good to them that love God." It is for God to determine when we can lay aside our tasks and receive their reward. Ours but to keep working at them till the evening come.

We are justified, indeed, we are obligated, to work and build for the future. Our present vocation is to plan and to carry out the earthly projects to which we are prompted by the Holy Spirit. At the same time, we must constantly recognize that the world will not last forever. The saga of earth which had a beginning will also have an end. How and when we do not know. But Christ will eventually come in glory. Then heaven and earth shall pass away and all the souls who have ever lived will be summoned to the final Judgment.

For centuries, that closing scene of the earthly drama captured the imagination of Christians and it has been depicted again and again. Of late, however, it has become unfashionable. A reaction against a literal interpretation of its imagery has resulted in a repudiation of the truth it seeks to portray. This is most unfortunate. For although angels may not have wings nor devils horns, though heaven is not a collection of billowy clouds nor hell a pit of fire and brimstone, there are the two alternatives of eternal bliss and eternal damnation; and each soul will be consigned to whichever he has chosen by his manner of life on earth.

The souls who have already been judged at death will not escape the Last Judgment, at which their irrevocable sentence will be proclaimed. Each soul will stand before Christ and before the whole company of men and angels and will be revealed in his true colors. The sickly yellow of pride, the blotchy purple of anger, the livid green of envy, the slimy grey of sloth, the sordid brown of avarice, the billious orange of gluttony, the fevered crimson of lust will be apparent for all to see. Woe to the soul who has but a few rags and tatters of his own accomplishments and his good intentions with which to cover his shame.

But blessed he who, whatever his sins may have been, has washed himself and made himself white in the Blood of the Immaculate Lamb. His brightness will outshine the sun. The courts of heaven will celebrate his triumph. Reclothed in his resurrection body, he will be united with all the redeemed in endless glory and will feed on the inexhaustible treasures of God's infinite love.

That is the destiny which God has prepared for you and me. We were created to know and to enjoy Him forever.

When the human race fell by sin, God in Christ pursued us to win us back. He gave His life for us men and for our salvation. He rose from the dead to bring us the fruits of His victory. Through the Gospel He calls us to be saints. In His Body the Church, He takes us by the hand to lead us to the Father. "Fear not, little flock," He assures us, "it is your Father's good pleasure to give you the Kingdom."

Though we must all stand before the Judgment Seat, we need not be afraid. For the Judge is none other than our Lord and Saviour Jesus Christ. He knows us and He loves us better than we love ourselves. If in this life we have sought to know Him, if we have become living members of His Body the Church, if we have participated in His life of worship and prayer, if we have repudiated our sins by humble and honest penitence, if we have surrendered our bodies to His gentle yoke of discipline and mortification, if we have let His Holy Spirit lead us into all truth, if we have done our duty in that state of life to which we have been called, then, when we are ushered into the presence of the Risen Christ, we shall be greeted with the eternal radiance of His approving smile. Then will our hearts be glad, when we see the Lord.